D0233640

NATIONAL PORTRAIT GALLERY

A VISITOR'S GUIDE

NATIONAL
PORTRAIT
GALLERY

A VISITOR'S GUIDE

John Cooper

Published in Great Britain by
National Portrait Gallery Publications
National Portrait Gallery
St Martin's Place
London WC2H OHE

ISBN 1 85514 298 8

A catalogue record for this book is available
from the British Library.

Editor: Susie Foster
Designer: Philip Lewis
Printed by Conti Tipocolor, Italy

The publisher would like to thank the copyright holders for
granting permission to reproduce works illustrated in this book.
Every effort has been made to contact the holders of copyright
material, and any omissions will be corrected in future editions
if the publisher is notified in writing.

Frontispiece: © Andrew Putler; page 76: on loan from the Tate Gallery © Tate,
London 2001; © Estate of Gwen John 2001. All rights reserved, DACS; page 94:
© Estate of Walter R. Sickert 2001. All rights reserved, DACS; page 97: By
Courtesy of the Estate of Patrick Heron/DACS/NPG; page 98: © The Andy
Warhol Foundation for the Visual Arts, Inc./ARS, NY and DACS, London 2001;
page 99: © Tom Wood; page 100: © Helmut Newton; page 102: © Gerald Scarfe;
page 104: © Maggi Hambling; page 107: © Stephen Finer; page 117: © Reserved;
page 119: © Tim O'Sullivan; page 120: © Marty St James.

All other works copyright © National Portrait Gallery, London 2001.

For a complete catalogue of current publications, please write to
the address above, or visit our website at www.npg.org.uk/pubs

Front cover (top to bottom): Mary Wollstonecraft, c.1797 (detail); Charles I, 1628
(detail); Isaac Rosenberg, 1915 (detail); Horatio Nelson, Viscount Nelson,
1800 (detail); Sir Nathaniel Bacon, c.1625 (detail); George Gordon Byron,
6th Baron Byron, 1813 (detail).

Back cover: Louise de Kéroualle, Duchess of Portsmouth, 1682 (detail).

Frontispiece: the early twentieth-century collection at the National
Portrait Gallery. (Photograph by Andrew Putler, www.andrewputler.com)

Preface

This book is intended to be a general introduction to the Gallery's permanent collection. The five centuries the collection covers have a section apiece and weave into a coherent historical narrative some of our most interesting personalities and their portraits. The selection represents the wide range of works of art, in terms of style, technique and aesthetic sophistication, which can be seen on our walls as well as those that are more in the way of personal favourites. The text follows the chronological and thematic arrangement of the Gallery's rooms, and is supplemented by a section on the most important media used to make portraits, written by a non-practitioner for non-practitioners. The *Visitor's Guide* ends with information on opening times and details of facilities and resources within the Gallery.

The Gallery responds generously to requests from other museums for loans, so you may find that occasionally another portrait has been substituted for one referred to in the text. All works illustrated in the *Visitor's Guide* are highlighted in the index in bold.

John Cooper
HEAD OF EDUCATION

The National Portrait Gallery

T HE NATIONAL PORTRAIT GALLERY effectively came into being on 2 December 1856 when the first Government Grant-in-Aid, £2,000, was allocated to our founding Trustees. The justification for this expenditure of public money was articulated by the then Prime Minister Lord Palmerston (1784–1865):

> There could be no greater incentive to mental exertion, to noble actions, to good conduct on the part of the living than for them to see before them the features of those who have done things which are worthy of our admiration, and whose example we are more induced to imitate when they are brought before us in the visible and tangible shape of portraits.

With these paternalistic words ringing in their ears, the Trustees set themselves 'to look to the celebrity of the person represented rather than to the merit of the artist' when acquiring portraits. From the start, though, they took a view of celebrity tempered by human fallibility, accepting that 'great faults and errors' should not exclude individuals from inclusion. To avoid rushing into judgement on the reputations of potential subjects, the Trustees ruled that persons could not be considered until they had been dead ten years, unless they were the reigning sovereign or his or her consort.

While Palmerston's lapidary statement and the Trustees' rules have been somewhat modified – the Gallery has admitted living sitters since 1969 – they still form the guiding principles of the institution. On alternate Wednesdays the curators meet to consider portraits directly on offer or passing through the salerooms and auction houses. The sitters' contribution to British life is assessed before the aesthetic qualities and art-historical context of the images are discussed. The portraits accepted then come up before the Trustees for ratification, which is in most cases granted.

The most important modifications to the original purpose have been the broadening of what constitutes a significant contribution, and the increasing

Henry VIII (1491–1547)
Detail of portrait illustrated on page 13.

Germaine Greer (b.1939)
Paula Rego, 1995. Pastel on paper laid on aluminium, 1200 × 1111mm (47 × 43¾")
(NPG 6351)

importance given to art and art history, leading to a recognition of the
Gallery's role as a place to learn about the art of portraiture since 1500.
The Gallery now works to two aims, which are worth quoting in full:

> To promote through the medium of portraits the appreciation and
> understanding of the men and women who have made and are making
> British history and culture.

> To promote the appreciation and understanding of portraiture in all media.

The Gallery seeks to understand more than to celebrate. While Lord
Palmerston wanted his contemporaries to gaze at, admire and then try to
emulate the men and women portrayed, the National Portrait Gallery of

today would hope to encourage thoughts about the complexity of human motivation – especially what drives individuals to seek positions of eminence – and to look at portraits as functions of that process. The Gallery also seeks to encourage the study and enjoyment of portraiture quite independently of any need to consider the reputation of the sitter. This is manifested partly in a greater and more informed attention to aesthetic matters in the initial consideration of portraits for purchase, and also through the development of a comprehensive temporary exhibition programme, much of which is driven by aesthetic and art-historical issues.

The main building was opened in 1896, forty years after the foundation of the institution. After an initial period at 29 Great George Street, Westminster, the collection was moved to South Kensington in 1870, and after a fire, to Bethnal Green in 1885 before a donation by W. H. Alexander, a rich property owner and benefactor of the arts, provided a permanent home. In 1933, the generosity of another benefactor, Lord Duveen (1869–1939) enabled the Gallery to open a wing running along Orange Street. The accommodation was always insufficient for the growing permanent and reference collections. By the mid-1980s, visitor numbers were increasing significantly, and by 1994 the Gallery achieved over one million visitors, due to the opening of the new twentieth century gallery. This success was repeated again in 1998 with visitors topping one million. Display space was totally inadequate, and more office space was also desperately needed. A public appeal, supported eloquently by Mrs Thatcher at its inception in 1989, and with Mrs Drue Heinz DBE as a prominent donor, enabled the Gallery to open the Archive and Library, new twentieth century galleries, education facilities and office accommodation in 1993.

In May 2000, thanks to the Heritage Lottery Fund, and to a small number of private donors, particularly Dr Christopher Ondaatje, a new National Portrait Gallery building was added in the space between ourselves and the National Gallery. This means that we can at last offer a high standard of public facilities: a roof-top restaurant, a state-of-the-art lecture theatre, an improved bookshop and a welcoming entrance hall supported by an information technology gallery, as well as two floors of new display space. It would be unwise to say that the Gallery is now complete – an active and energetic institution has a built-in tendency to expand – but the national collection of portraits is now housed in excellent conditions, and has been made as accessible as possible for the new millennium.

Second Floor

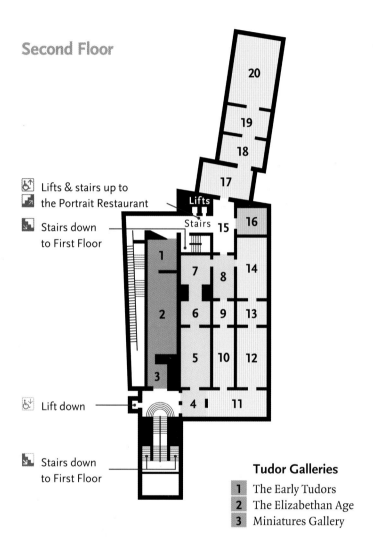

Lifts & stairs up to
the Portrait Restaurant

Stairs down
to First Floor

Lifts

Stairs

Lift down

Stairs down
to First Floor

Tudor Galleries

1 The Early Tudors
2 The Elizabethan Age
3 Miniatures Gallery

Sixteenth Century: The Tudors

T HE EARLIEST authenticated painted portraits in the Gallery date from the Tudor period. Henry Tudor claimed the throne as Henry VII after the Battle of Bosworth in 1485, at which his predecessor and rival Richard III was killed. The battle was the last in a dynastic struggle known as The Wars of the Roses which had endured for much of the fifteenth century. Two branches of the Plantagenet family, the descendants of the Dukes of York and Lancaster, whose symbols were the white and red rose respectively, fought for the privilege of being the line of royal succession. The Battle of Bosworth decided the issue, with the senior Lancastrian, Henry Tudor, defeating Richard III, formerly Duke of York.

Richard III was a controversial figure in his own time and his subsequent reputation has remained a matter of vigorous discussion, fuelled by

Richard III (1452–85)
Unknown artist, *c.*1570–99
Oil on panel, 638 × 470mm
(25⅛ × 18½")
(NPG 148)

Henry VII (1457–1509)
Unknown artist, 1505
Oil on panel, 425 × 305mm (16¾ × 12")
(NPG 416)

Shakespeare's play and its later theatrical and cinematic reinterpretations, by a corpus of academic and imaginative literature, by folk-memory, and by passionate advocacy from committed 'Ricardians'. Portraits have been a key element of this discourse: that illustrated on page 11 was probably produced late in the sixteenth century; if Richard's face shows any expression, it is anxious, rather than evil or forceful.

Henry VII married Elizabeth of York as a conciliatory gesture: the Tudor rose, a blend of the red of Lancaster and the white of York, became a symbol of their position as peacemakers, and makes many appearances in

Henry VII and Henry VIII (1457–1509 and 1491–1547)
Hans Holbein, c.1536–7
Ink and watercolour on paper,
2578 × 1372mm (101½ × 54")
(NPG 4027)

This is a detailed preparatory drawing, or 'cartoon', for the left-hand side of a large dynastic mural in Whitehall Palace depicting Henry VIII, accompanied by his third wife Jane Seymour, and Henry's parents Henry VII and Elizabeth of York. Holbein used black ink and pricked through, or 'pounced', the paper to transfer the outlines to the wall. The mural was destroyed when Whitehall Palace was burned down in 1698.

Cardinal Thomas Wolsey (1475–1530)
Unknown artist, c.1570–99
Oil on panel, 838 × 559mm (33 × 22")
(NPG 32)

portraits. The Gallery's most well-known portrait of Henry, as the contemporary inscription says, dates from 1505, and exemplifies a key function of portraiture in providing information for the parties involved in marriage contracts. Elizabeth of York had died in 1503, and Henry aspired to a prestigious second marriage to Margaret of Austria, the daughter of Maximilian I, the Holy Roman Emperor. The inscription says that the portrait was commissioned by Hermann Rinck, who was the Emperor's agent. The artist has given us a vivid image of a sharp-faced monarch whose appearance may have caused Margaret some apprehension. There was no marriage.

Hans Holbein's great image of Henry VII and Henry VIII (page 13) had a much broader and more prestigious function: to express the security of the

Catherine Parr (1512–48)
Attributed to Master John, c.1545
Oil on panel, 1803 × 940mm (71 × 37")
(NPG 4451)

Once thought to show Lady Jane Grey, we are now certain that this is Catherine Parr, based on the study of royal jewel lists, one from 1542, one from 1550, and one undated. These show that the crown-headed jewel worn on her breast belonged to Catherine and the girdle of cameos may have been inherited from Catherine Howard. Lady Jane Grey is unlikely to have had access to these jewels.

Sir Thomas More, his Father, his Household and his Descendants

ROWLAND LOCKEY, partly after
Hans Holbein, 1593

Oil on canvas, 2274 × 3302mm
(89½ × 130")
(NPG 2765)

It was a happy coincidence that this picture was acquired by the Gallery in 1935, exactly 400 years after the execution by Henry VIII of Sir Thomas More, and in the year of his canonisation.

In the early 1590s, Sir Thomas More's grandson, Thomas More II, was living at Lower Leyton in Essex; the family were 'recusants', those whose continuing loyalty to the Roman Catholic Church made it impossible for them to accept the communion of the Church of England. This painting was surely conceived as a defiant pictorial genealogy, a family tree in paint, emphasising the More family's loyalty to the old faith.

Five generations of the family are represented in the picture. On the extreme left is **(1)** Sir John More (1451–1530), father of the famous Sir Thomas. Next is Anne Cresacre (1511–77), a ward of Sir Thomas (under his legal protection) then **(2)** Sir Thomas himself (1478–1535), and **(3)** his son John (1510–47) who married Anne. Sir Thomas's three daughters Cecily Heron (b.1507), Elizabeth Dauncey (b.1506) and Margaret Roper (1505–44) appear next. Then comes **(4)** Thomas More II (1531–1606) seated next to his wife Maria Scrope (1534–1607), with **(5)** two of their sons: the eldest, John (1557–99), and the youngest, the beardless Christopher Cresacre More (1572–1649) behind. The portrait above Christopher is of his grandmother Anne in about 1560.

It seems that in 1590, Thomas More II acquired Hans Holbein's painting of the family of Sir Thomas More made c.1527–8 (since destroyed). He then commissioned Rowland Lockey to make three versions of it: one, a more or less exact copy of the original, now at Nostell Priory (National Trust, near Wakefield), and two in which Thomas More II's own family (generations **4** and **5**) is represented alongside generations **1** to **3** centred on Sir Thomas More. The National Portrait Gallery's large picture is one of these two, while the other is a miniature version, now in the Victoria and Albert Museum.

For the Gallery's picture, Lockey copied

generations **1** to **3** from Holbein's work, retaining the poses but moving Elizabeth from between her grandfather and an adopted sister so that she stands awkwardly between her blood-sisters. Lockey then added the new portraits of Thomas More II and his family. To make room, and maintain the genealogical theme, acting presumably with his patron's approval, he dropped from Holbein's line-up non-family members, or those who, like Sir Thomas More's *second* wife Dame Alice (on the extreme right in the Nostell group), made no procreative contribution.

The meaning of the picture is clear: here is a family, cultured, well-read, armigerous (having coats-of-arms), the later generations worthy successors to Sir Thomas in their proud Catholicism. This they show by the red prayer books, the crucifix on Maria's chest, and the cross worn by the grandmother they honour by means of a portrait. Further religious significance is probably carried by the flowers, particularly the white Madonna Lily on the extreme left. The extensive inscription in Latin, a later addition, gives the names and dates of the sitters.

Tudor dynasty and the magnificence of the younger king's person. Henry VII appears posthumously as the venerable progenitor of the mighty son, the contrasting moods evoked by the body-language of the figures. Henry VIII is depicted as the great Renaissance prince, powerful enough to replace the authority of the Pope over the English Church, and a worthy rival of both Francis I of France and the Holy Roman Emperor Charles V. Holbein was probably engaged on the work during 1536–7, and may well have obtained the commission through the influence of Thomas Cromwell, whom he had painted previously and whose energy and ruthlessness had established the administrative and legal structure of the break with papal authority. Cromwell's portrait in the Gallery is a copy after Holbein, exemplifying the process by which so many surviving sixteenth-century portraits were made. The survival of face patterns, templates from which standard images could be worked up, such as the one of Bishop John Fisher, suggests that a system of production existed to satisfy the increasing demand for famous faces. Other examples of good copies after Holbein are the portraits of Archbishop William Warham and Nicholas Kratzer. It is a pity that Holbein never painted Cardinal Thomas Wolsey; however, the Gallery's portrait of him (page 15) does show his power and bulk.

If art historians have to develop a fine eye for establishing the relative merits of copies in terms of their relation to the work of a particular artist, they also have to resolve questions about the identity of the sitters. The portrait of Catherine Parr (page 14), Henry VIII's last wife, was acquired for the Gallery as Lady Jane Grey (the 'nine days queen'). Subsequent in-depth research into the ownership of the jewels depicted has led to the present identification.

The break with Rome under Henry VIII, consolidated under Edward VI, reversed under Mary I and finally secured under Elizabeth I was not achieved without casualties. Sir Thomas More's refusal to accept the supremacy of Henry VIII over the Church led to his trial and execution, engineered by Thomas Cromwell. The portrait of *Sir Thomas More, his Father, his Household and his Descendants*, commissioned by Sir Thomas More's grandson in 1592, demonstrates the family's refusal to renounce Roman Catholicism despite the fines and restrictions of civil liberty imposed upon 'recusants'.

Archbishop Thomas Cranmer, as depicted meticulously by Gerlach Flicke, certainly appears as a great prince of the Church, but essentially of a Protestant one, surrounded by books and wearing a plain white surplice.

Thomas Cranmer (1489–1556)
Gerlach Flicke, 1546. Oil on panel, 984 × 762mm (38¾ × 30")
(NPG 535)

Having secured for Henry his divorce from Anne Boleyn, Cranmer
survived the vagaries of the monarch's temper, served his son Edward,
but was burned for heresy under Mary I. Fellow sufferers, Bishops Latimer
and Ridley, are also represented in the Gallery. Cranmer appears in
another painting suffused with the religious controversy of the time,
Edward VI and the Pope.

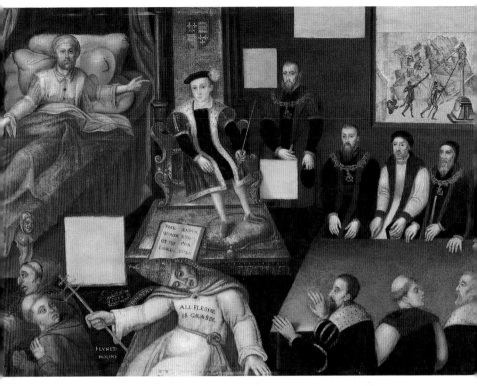

Edward VI (1537–53) **and the Pope: an Allegory of the Reformation**
Unknown artist, *c.*1570
Oil on panel, 622 × 908mm (24½ × 35¾")
(NPG 4165)

Until recently, this painting was thought to date from Edward's reign, and
to be a comment on the further protestantisation of the Church; it has now
been convincingly shown that it dates from the reign of Elizabeth I, and
was addressed to the queen and her government as a reminder of the
appropriate direction the church settlement should take. Research has
demonstrated that the strikingly unusual depiction of key objects such as
Henry VIII's bedpost and the collapsed building in the scene of iconoclasm
at top right was borrowed from a Dutch source not available before the
mid-1560s.

The young king Edward VI is also represented in a full-length portrait by
an unknown artist. He appears with juvenile assurance and assumes the
confident posture established by his father as appropriate for a male ruler.
More curiously, his profile is shown in the 'Anamorphosis' by William
Scrots, a playful experiment with the physics of visual perception which
must have amused him and his young companions. Viewed from the front

as a distorted profile, when seen through an aperture in the side of the frame the portrait appears as a normal face.

Mary I has a somewhat grim reputation in popular history as a hard-faced persecutor of Protestants, unloved bride of Philip II of Spain and unhappy loser of England's last French possession, Calais. The portrait of her by Hans Eworth presents a more sympathetic image, possibly a flattering one of the artist's most important patron. Eworth, from the Netherlands, spent some thirty years in England, producing highly competent portraits, sumptuous in expensive detail, but not without psychological interest. His double portrait of Mary Neville, Lady Dacre, and her son Gregory Fiennes, 10th Baron Dacre is a splendid study of a formidable matriarch, whose role in re-establishing the family's honour after the execution of the 9th Lord Dacre – for taking part in a poaching expedition in which he was an accessory to the murder of a gamekeeper – is thus commemorated. Here a noble family uses a portrait to reassert its prestige. It is sad to relate, however, that Gregory is said to have been 'a little Crack-brain'd'.

The early portraits of Elizabeth I are relatively conventional presentations. The *Coronation Portrait* shows her in a fine cloth-of-gold robe, previously worn by Mary I, and displays the twenty-six-year-old queen in the stylised, or

Mary I (1516–58)
Hans Eworth, 1554
Oil on panel, 216 × 169mm (8½ × 6⅝")
(NPG 4861)

Mary, Queen of Scots (1542–87)
Unknown artist after Nicholas Hilliard, c.1610
Oil on panel, 791 × 902mm (31⅛ × 35½")
(NPG 429)

hieratic, manner already well-established by the sixteenth century as appropriate for monarchs in state. It is intriguing that dendrochronology, the science of tree-ring dating, suggests that the panel on which it is painted may date from the end of the century; the image was perhaps part of the rejuvenating of the ageing queen by means of flattering and ever-youthful portraits. The portrait of her dating from 1575, with the curiously looped pearls, is an image of dignity and some severity, but understated in terms of its royal message. From the mid-1580s the story becomes more complex: Elizabeth, now in her mid-fifties, was no longer marriageable, and in 1570 had been excommunicated by the Pope as her country was clearly irretrievably heretical. This position of potential weakness, an unmarried female ruler, and a defiantly Protestant one increasingly threatened by the crusading zeal of Philip II (whose choice as replacement monarch was the Roman Catholic Mary, Queen of Scots) needed the boost of a favourable spin. Elizabeth and her advisers realised that portraits could, to some extent, provide this, and so emerged a series of images in which the singularity of the queen became a strength, her virginity a symbol of her sacrifice of personal gratification for the national good. Initially aimed at the ruling élite and their foreign counterparts, by the end of her reign relatively cheap engravings were conveying her image to a wider public. The portrait of Elizabeth standing on a map, known as the 'Ditchley Portrait' after the country house in Oxfordshire owned by Sir Henry Lee, who commissioned it, is a remarkable essay in both coded and clear messages, in public and private expression.

Lee was just one among many ambitious, talented arriviste courtiers whose loyalty Elizabeth needed to secure. She could always rely on William Cecil, 1st Baron Burghley and his son Robert Cecil, 1st Earl of Salisbury, whose measured advice was crucial to the generally successful conduct of

Elizabeth I (1533–1603)
Marcus Gheeraerts the Younger, c.1592
Oil on canvas, 2413 × 1524mm (95 × 60")
(NPG 2561)

The 'Ditchley Portrait', depicts the mighty queen, her power both earthly and cosmic, dominating England. More personally, in Latin tags and the sonnet on the right, Sir Henry Lee expresses both admiration and gratitude at her forgiveness of him for living at Ditchley, Oxfordshire with his mistress, when his first allegiance in love, according to the manners of the court, was to the fair Eliza.

domestic and foreign policy. These deep-thinking, sagacious men contrasted with more flamboyant performers such as Robert Dudley, 2nd Earl of Leicester, and his stepson Robert Devereux, 2nd Earl of Essex, to whose good looks and charisma the queen was attracted. Leicester, for example, described as a 'light and greedy man', was the only Englishman she seriously considered marrying; William Cecil, considering such a match disastrous, used all his formidable powers as an intriguer to prevent it. Later William's son, Robert Cecil, took a leading part in the destruction of Essex, whose rash and injudicious rebellion in 1601 led him to the scaffold. The Cecils, Leicester and Essex were all ambitious men, acutely aware of the importance of wealth and connection, and of the part portraits played in demonstrating their high status at court. The quieter, deeper ways of the Cecils proved the more

Robert Devereux, 2nd Earl of Essex (1566–1601)
Attributed to Nicholas Hilliard, c.1587
Miniature on vellum, 248 × 203mm (9¾ × 8") (NPG 6241)

Sir Francis Drake (1540–96)
Unknown artist, c.1580
Oil on panel, 1813 × 1130mm (71⅜ × 44½") (NPG 4032)

enduring; 400 years later their descendants still occupy the great houses at Burghley and Hatfield, built on the profits of their service.

Sir Walter Ralegh and Sir Francis Drake are represented by portraits which perhaps reflect their relative degrees of courtly sophistication. Ralegh, explorer and naval commander though he was, can also be counted as one of the queen's favourites, equally at home with sonnets and pavans as he was with cordage and quadrants. The Gallery's portrait of him with his son has a degree of refinement lacking in the cruder image of Drake. Drake was no courtier, but the most dangerous naval opponent of Philip II, whose prowess was recognised in his own time by the demand for portraits of him both at home and abroad. Even Pope Sixtus V, irritated by Philip's prevarication over preparing the Armada against England, held Drake up to him as an example of effective action. The portrait of Drake (page 25) has suffered harsh treatment over the years; the head and shoulders section was, at one stage, detached from the rest, as a close viewing shows. Recent examination suggests that the larger section may have been a later addition altogether.

William Shakespeare, like Drake, was admired at the court, but not of it. Now acknowledged as one of the great figures of world literature, there is a disappointing lack of striking images to reflect this. The rather stodgy

William Shakespeare
(1564–1616)
Attributed to John Taylor, c.1610
Oil on canvas, 552 × 438mm
(21¾ × 17¼") (NPG 1)

The Somerset House Conference, 1604
Unknown artist, 1604. Oil on canvas, 2057 × 2680mm (81 × 105½") (NPG 665)

monument in Holy Trinity Church at Stratford, the awkward engraving by
Martin Droeshout from the First Folio, of which the Gallery has a later
edition, and the modest oil painting shown here are the only three images
with a reasonable claim to have been produced at least under the auspices
of people who knew him. The Gallery's painting, the first portrait acquired
after its foundation in 1856, has an intriguing but secure enough provenance,
traceable back to Shakespeare's godson William Davenant.

The long war against Spain was brought to a close in 1604 by the Treaty
of London thrashed out at the Somerset House Conference. Elizabeth I had
died the previous year, and her cousin James VI of Scotland had succeeded
her as James I. The Tudor monarchy had established England; it was now
up to the Stuarts to see what they could do for Britain.

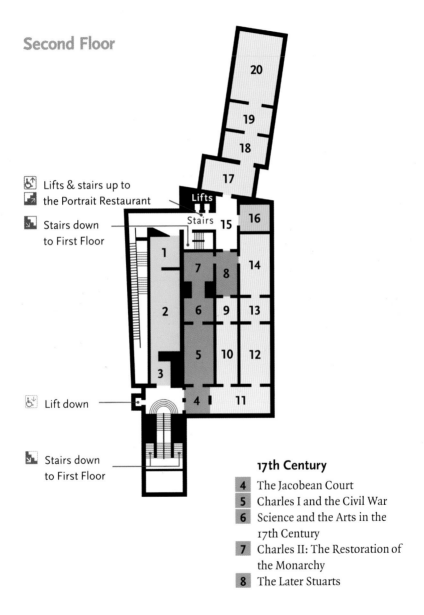

Second Floor

Lifts & stairs up to
the Portrait Restaurant

Stairs down
to First Floor

Lifts

Stairs

Lift down

Stairs down
to First Floor

17th Century

4 The Jacobean Court
5 Charles I and the Civil War
6 Science and the Arts in the
   17th Century
7 Charles II: The Restoration of
   the Monarchy
8 The Later Stuarts

Seventeenth Century: The Stuarts

KING JAMES I came down from Scotland determined to enjoy the fruits of a richer and less dangerous kingdom than the land he had left. He had done well to survive, but in so doing had not learned any of the public style and graceful expression of the great queen he replaced.

James had little interest in his own image and it was with difficulty that he was made to sit for his portrait. He believed passionately in the divine right of monarchs to rule, but preferred to express his beliefs verbally and in cogent texts rather than through imagery.

This could not be said for his great favourite, the much-portrayed George Villiers, Duke of Buckingham. Buckingham was spectacularly good-looking, charismatic, charming and courtly; James I was besotted, and promoted the young man so rapidly – 'more a flight than a growth' said the disapproving Lord Clarendon – that within four years of his appointment as gentleman of the bedchamber in 1615 he was a Marquess, Lord High Admiral and the virtual ruler of the country. There are many handsome portraits of him; that attributed to William Larkin (page 30), displays his beauty and status in all its uncompromising and ostentatious splendour. Stylistically as much Elizabethan as Jacobean, and sometimes referred to as Jacobethan, it also has elements of the courtly mannerist style in which elongation and exaggeration of the vertical is intended to convey refinement and elegance. Buckingham wears his robes as a Knight of the Order of the Garter, the highest order of chivalry forming an élite group around the sovereign, and allows the front to fall open to display a prodigious length of leg.

The portrait makes an interesting comparison with that of Thomas Howard, 2nd Earl of Arundel and Surrey (page 31): this is a lively study by Peter Paul Rubens, a dress-rehearsal for a three-quarter-length portrait now in the Isabella Stewart Gardner Museum (Boston, Mass.). The contrast exemplifies the sea-change in style which occurred once England had been fully opened up to continental aesthetic influences under the early Stuarts. Arundel is all baroque vigour, living flesh and hard metal with the light moulding his form and adding drama to his presence. It renders archaic the

Thomas Howard, 2nd Earl of Arundel and Surrey (1585–1646)
Sir Peter Paul Rubens, 1629
Oil on canvas, 686 × 533mm
(27 × 21") (NPG 2391)

strange elongations and even lighting of Buckingham's picture. Both men were avid collectors and patrons of Rubens and his compatriot Anthony van Dyck; while Arundel was the more scholarly and discriminating, Buckingham particularly enjoyed the associated splendour and enhanced personal prestige.

The two sons of James I were both significant patrons of all forms of art. Henry Frederick, Prince of Wales, by the time of his premature death at the age of eighteen in 1612 had, with the guidance of the great professional Inigo Jones, as well as the courtly amateurs described above, amassed a fine collection. His younger brother, later Charles I, in complete contrast to his

George Villiers, 1st Duke of Buckingham (1592–1628)
Attributed to William Larkin, c.1616
Oil on canvas, 2057 × 1194mm (81 × 47")
(NPG 3840)

This splendid portrait has undergone some changes. Acquired by the Gallery with the background curtains painted green, it was so displayed until 1985, when close examination revealed fragments of paint of the present colour which under analysis proved to be the original. Skilfully restored to its full glory, by removing the green paint and matching the fragments, we can now enjoy the voluptuous splendour of its original colour scheme.

The Capel Family
Cornelius Johnson, c.1640
Oil on canvas, 1600 × 2591mm (63 × 102") (NPG 4759)

father James I, while mentally inflexible and diffident, had a highly
developed sense of how art could promote his person and his beliefs. It was
he who brought Van Dyck to England in 1632; to see the result for Charles
personally, visit the National Gallery to view the great equestrian portrait.
In the National Portrait Gallery you can see Charles's cousin Lord George
Stuart, 9th Seigneur d'Aubigny, disguised by Van Dyck as a shepherd
yearning for his nymph. Van Dyck's brilliance inspired emulation: the four
central figures of The Capel Family by Cornelius Johnson are a direct borrowing
from Van Dyck's portrait of the royal family of 1632 in the Royal Collection.

The portrait of Charles I by Gerard Honthorst is a sensitive portrayal of
the young king, quite possibly a study for the great Hampton Court allegory
Mercury Presenting the Liberal Arts to Apollo and Diana, which features Charles I
as Apollo. Charles I and Queen Henrietta Maria enjoyed both watching and
taking part in masques (a performance of dance, drama and music with, as
the 1630s progressed, increasingly political overtones).

Charles I (1600–49)
Gerard Honthorst, 1628
Oil on canvas, 762 × 641mm (30 × 25¼")
(NPG 4444)

Thought to be a study for the great Hampton Court allegorical painting
in which Charles as Apollo, accompanied by Henrietta Maria as Diana,
receives the Duke of Buckingham as Mercury, who introduces the Liberal
Arts. Charles took a lively interest in the meaning of masques, finding
solace in the symbolic destruction of allegorical characters such as
'Jealousy' and 'Discord' as real political difficulties intruded into his life in
the late 1630s.

Oliver Cromwell (1599–1658)
Samuel Cooper, 1649
Miniature, watercolour on vellum,
57 × 48mm (2¼ × 1⅞") (NPG 5589)

The language of allegory is also employed in Van Dyck's portrait of Lady Venetia Digby. This image is probably posthumous. Venetia Stanley married the gallant Sir Kenelm Digby, son of the Gunpowder plotter Sir Everard and also a Roman Catholic; to be a Catholic at the court of Charles I was both fashionable and, in terms of the aesthetic associations of the religion, highly acceptable to Charles I.

The plain image of Oliver Cromwell by Samuel Cooper is as far from a complex baroque allegory as you can get. This miniature, painted in watercolour on vellum, was only recently identified as Cromwell, and is now accepted as the earliest authentic portrait of the only commoner to have been our Head of State. It dates from 1649, the year of the trial and execution of Charles I which Cromwell did so much to bring about. Cooper's close association with Cromwell, his family and other leading Parliamentarians does not seem to have militated against his employment by Charles II and his court after the restoration of the monarchy in 1660.

The political and social upheavals of the English Civil Wars produced a mass of polemical and theoretical explanation and justification. Thomas Hobbes's contribution was *Leviathan* (1651) in which he argued the necessity of arbitrary power, specifically royal power, to bring order to a chaotic world in which the life of man was 'nasty, brutish and short'. This portrait by John Michael Wright is a splendid image of a cantankerous, rather timid old intellectual. Wright is an interesting artist, somewhat overshadowed by the reputations of his more glamorous contemporaries, and it is worth considering his versatility by looking at three further portraits: a complex

Thomas Hobbes (1588–1679)
John Michael Wright, *c*.1669–70
Oil on canvas, 660 × 546mm (26 × 21½") (NPG 225)

allegory woven around Elizabeth Claypole (née Cromwell) and her father;
a gauche attempt at sexiness in depicting Charles II's mistress Barbara
Palmer, Duchess of Cleveland; and Wright's portrait of the family of
Sir Robert Vyner, full of solid materialism, but also psychological interest
in the forthright mother, perky daughter, cherished son and cute dog.
Sir Robert, somewhat overshadowed in the painting, might be seen as having
intimations of his future bankruptcy and the sad death of the boy, Charles,
in 1688, aged twenty-two.

Venetia, Lady Digby (1600–33)

SIR ANTHONY VAN DYCK, c.1633–4

Oil on canvas, 1011 × 802mm (39¾ × 31½")
(NPG 5727)

In her youth Venetia Stanley acquired a reputation for promiscuity, which her husband Sir Kenelm Digby was anxious to replace with something more acceptable, particularly as his family had opposed the marriage because of her alleged moral laxity. An erudite man, he used his extensive knowledge of mythology and allegory to put together a convincing brief for his friend, the artist Anthony van Dyck, to develop into a pictorial refutation of the rumours about her. Van Dyck himself was no great allegorist, but was content to follow the desires of the man who was 'always his most generous friend and protector'.

To help him to fulfil Digby's plan, Van Dyck probably consulted Cesare Ripa's well-known reference book *Iconologia*, which had been available in illustrated editions since 1603. In this he would have found both *Prudenza* with a serpent encircling her arm and a representation of *Castita* (Charity) with a Cupid subdued beneath her feet. He then arranged the allegorical references in a clear design: if you draw a diagonal line from the top-left corner to the bottom right, everything to the right is good and all to the left is bad. Lady Digby has overcome all the evil and achieved the serenity of redemption as the little angels crown her victory. Two-faced Deceit, coarse, rough and tawny, unlike her milky purity, cowers impotently with bound hands, symbolising the defeat of 'that monster which was begot of some fiend in hell', as Digby said of the 'false construction' put on her character. With a disdainful foot she dismisses Cupid, the symbol of lust whose flaming torch gutters to ashes. Her left hand rests approvingly on one of two turtle doves, symbols of married love, while her right holds a snake, a symbol of wisdom (although to most people these days the connotations of snakes are negative!).

Although Venetia appears to be the mistress of her own redemption, Digby would expect to share in the credit. He had, after all, according to John Aubrey, claimed that he 'could take a woman out of a whorehouse and make her honest'. It is highly likely, although not certain, that this painting was posthumous, or at least completed after her sudden death on 1 May 1633. Digby was devastated by his wife's demise; the most poignant memorial to her is the death-bed portrait, with a crushed rose on the counterpane, now in the Dulwich Picture Gallery, London.

Samuel Pepys (1633–1703)
John Hayls, 1666
Oil on canvas, 756 × 629mm
(29¾ × 24¾") (NPG 211)

Sir Robert was a goldsmith and made the coronation regalia for Charles II which appears in the dominating portrait of the king at the age of fifty attributed to Thomas Hawker. Charles preserved as much of the monarchy's power as he could after the ravages of the Civil War, employing his own subtlety and charm as well as generous subsidies from Louis XIV of France.

Samuel Pepys left us one of the great documents of English history. His diaries, covering the years 1660–69, are justly celebrated for their many-layered record of all aspects of public and private life, ranging from Pepys's successful career as an admiralty official to observations on the Duchess of Cleveland's underwear seen drying in the Privy Garden at Whitehall. The making of this portrait by John Hayls is faithfully recorded in the *Diary* during the early months of 1666, including Pepys's enthusiastic interference as the

Charles II (1630–85)
Attributed to Thomas Hawker, c.1680
Oil on canvas, 2267 × 1356mm (89¼ × 53⅜")
(NPG 4691)

This portrait bears close scrutiny: the fair hands and strangely articulated legs reveal something of the process of making such images, with everything below the chin being assembled somewhat piecemeal by assistants in the artist's studio; the face, though, is lively enough, and even bears a striking resemblance to the actor Walter Matthau!

Sir Peter Lely (1618–80)
Self-portrait, c.1660
Oil on canvas, 1080 × 876mm
(42½ × 34½")
(NPG 3897)

project proceeded. He wears a new wig and a fashionable gown of Madras silk, known as a banyan, then the ultimate in smart leisure-wear, hired specially for the portrait as he was not then in a position to buy one. Pepys's influence extended beyond the bounds of his professional career, for he was both an MP and President of the Royal Society. Talent he undoubtedly had, but he needed great men to bring him on: both Edward Montagu, 1st Earl of Sandwich and James Duke of York (later James II) were instrumental in his rise through the ranks of admiralty officials. The Gallery's portraits of these men are both the work of Sir Peter Lely, Dutch-born court painter to Charles II, who was active in England from the mid-1640s. Lely, whose self-portrait certainly bears out Pepys's description of him as 'a mighty proud man and full of state', both defined for contempories and reflected for posterity the extravagant personal style of the Restoration Court.

Pepys's *Diary* has been available in various editions since 1825, but it is less easy to get access to the works of John Wilmot, 2nd Earl of Rochester. Credited with the mock epitaph for Charles II,

> Here lies our sovereign lord the king
> Whose promise none relies on;

> He never said a foolish thing
> Nor ever did a wise one

Rochester's wit was more regularly employed in producing pornographic verse, some of it describing the king's own activities. Rochester's portrait is cynically self-deprecatory: the monkey, a symbol of vanity, rips up verse while crowned with laurels by the poet himself.

John Wilmot, 2nd Earl of Rochester (1647–80)
Unknown artist, c.1665–70. Oil on canvas, 1270 × 991mm (50 × 39") (NPG 804)

Rochester and other young men and women followed the tolerant code of sexual behaviour established by the king himself. Charles II had married Catherine of Braganza in 1660: her portrait shows a rather tentative sixteen-year-old, dressed in a Portuguese style that caused much amusement among the sophisticates at the English court. Later images show that she learned to dress fashionably. She also learned to accept that her husband had a series of glamorous mistresses, from whom fourteen children were produced while she was unable to bear live children. This fact precipitated a major constitutional crisis when James, Duke of York, the king's brother and successor in the absence of a legitimate heir, declared himself a Roman Catholic.

One of Charles II's most exotic mistresses was Louise de Kéroualle, Duchess of Portsmouth, seen here painted by Pierre Mignard. A Breton aristocrat, she was an attendant of Charles's sister Henrietta Anne, Duchess of Orleans, who lived in France, their mother's country, where she assiduously promoted the interests of her brother's kingdom. In 1670, as Charles cultivated closer relations with Louis XIV, Henrietta Anne came to England as part of a goodwill exercise which bore fruit in the Treaty of Dover, and Louise de Kéroualle was included in her entourage. This may have been a deliberate ploy to engage Charles in a romance and thus further cement Anglo-French relations. The result was a relationship that lasted until the king's death in 1685. He called her 'Fubbs' ('fubbsy' means pretty in a chubby-cheeked sort of way). Her great rival was the plebeian Nell Gwyn, whose robust manners and thespian histrionics provided a contrast to the elegant and courtly Frenchwoman.

Some way away from the sensuality and intrigue of the court was the world of John Bunyan. Although the Church of England had re-established its authority after the Restoration, the non-conformity stimulated by the

Louise de Kéroualle, Duchess of Portsmouth (1649–1734)
Pierre Mignard, 1682
Oil on canvas, 1207 × 953mm (47½ × 37½")
(NPG 497)

Light, bright and precise in contrast to the languid postures and suffused colour of English baroque portraits, this is a very French picture. The Duchess – Charles II's 'Catholic Whore' according to her rival Nell Gwyn – poses with her black servant to enhance her fashionably pallid complexion. The portrait may be mythologising her as the sea-nymph Thetis, an appropriate role for a Duchess of Portsmouth.

John Bunyan (1628–88)
Thomas Sadler, 1684
Oil on canvas, 749 × 635mm
(29½ × 25") (NPG 1311)

Anne (1665–1714)
Michael Dahl, 1705
Oil on canvas, 2368 × 1448mm
(93¼ × 57") (NPG 6187)

Civil Wars still had its influence in religious writing and unlicensed preaching. Bunyan practised both, and was imprisoned in Bedford gaol from 1660 to 1672. His masterpiece, *The Pilgrim's Progress*, was published in 1678; this powerful religious allegory of the victory of Faith over Corruption narrated in colourful yet accessible language became an influential text of political as well as religious radicalism.

King James II, having declared himself a Roman Catholic, succeeded to the throne in 1685 and the worst fears of the influential supporters of the Church of England were realised. Three years later, he was forced out and replaced by the Dutch William, Prince of Orange, who took the title William III, his legitimacy guaranteed by his Queen, Mary II, the Protestant elder daughter of James II. As King William III, he had access to the resources of Britain to supplement those of Holland in the struggle against his great enemy Louis XIV of France.

Queen Anne, James's younger daughter, was the last of the Stuarts, despite the prodigious efforts of her and her husband Prince George of Denmark to ensure the continuity of the line. The unfortunate woman became pregnant eighteen times, but only one of her children survived even into childhood. An Act of Succession was passed in 1701 to guarantee that

the heir to the throne would be her Protestant cousin Sophia of Hanover; the promoters of the Act wanted to avoid any chance of the Roman Catholic James Edward Stuart, son of James II, succeeding to the throne. Protégés of the French court, James Edward and his little sister Louisa can be seen in a portrait by Nicolas de Largillière, very much presented as royalty.

The supporters of James II's descendants were known as 'Jacobites', and were assisted by Louis XIV of France, involving Britain in a lengthy war in alliance with the Dutch. Anne's predecessor, William III, had already singled out John Churchill, 1st Duke of Marlborough, as his military heir in the struggle against France. Sarah Churchill, a formidable personality, was a long-standing favourite of Queen Anne, and had great influence over her thoughts and actions. Although this relationship turned sour, it contributed to the social and political elevation of the Marlboroughs. The duke won his battles, but also demonstrated diplomatic skills in sustaining the Grand Alliance, primarily with the Dutch and Austrians, the essential partnership for winning the conflict out of which Britain emerged as a great power.

John Churchill, 1st Duke of Marlborough (1650–1722)
Sir Godfrey Kneller, c.1706
Oil on canvas, 927 × 737mm (36½ × 29")
(NPG 902)

Second Floor

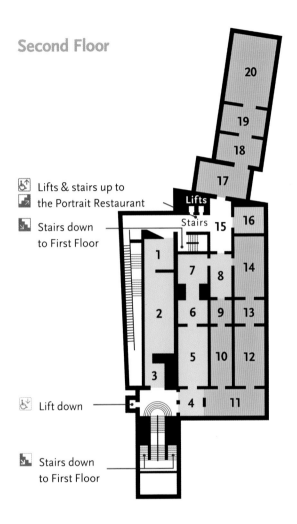

Lifts & stairs up to
the Portrait Restaurant

Stairs down
to First Floor

Lifts

Stairs

Lift down

Stairs down
to First Floor

18th Century

9 The Kit-cat Club
10 The Arts in the early 18th Century
11 Britain in the early 18th Century
12 The Arts in the later 18th Century
13 Science and Industry in the
    18th Century
14 Britain becomes a World Power

Late 18th and early 19th Century

17 Britain at War 1793–1815
18 The Romantics
19 Science and Industry in the
    early 19th Century
20 The Regency

Eighteenth Century: The Hanoverians

GEORGE I succeeded Anne in 1714; although Elector of Hanover and to all intents and purposes a German, he had a solid enough Protestant line of descent to qualify under the terms of the Act of Succession, and as a direct descendant of Charles I's sister Elizabeth, enough Stuart blood to mollify some of the potential opposition. Not all of it though: both James II's son James Edward Stuart and his grandson Charles Edward Stuart (Bonnie Prince Charlie) led Jacobite risings, in 1715 and 1745, against George I and his son George II. Although ill-conceived, inadequately supported by Britain's continental enemies, and dogged by bad luck, this Jacobite threat of restoring the Stuart monarchy was real enough until Charles Edward Stuart was defeated at the Battle of Culloden, near Inverness, in 1746.

The constitutional upheavals of the mid-seventeenth century onwards, the cost of the wars against France and the arrival as monarch of a foreign prince with continental interests and a shaky command of English provided the British aristocracy and their associates with opportunities for influence and executive power which were gratefully seized. Exemplifying this was Robert Walpole, 1st Earl of Orford. An East Anglian landowner, his formidable personality, strong intellect and calculating assessment of human motivation made him master of the House of Commons, and from 1721 to 1742, the first 'prime minister' of the Crown. His portrait from the studio of Jean Baptiste van Loo (page 51), a French artist fashionable in London in the late 1730s, shows something of the robust confidence of 'Cock Robin', as he was called.

The increasing prosperity of both agriculture and commerce created a new market for all forms of culture, less dependent on the court and its international connections. In many ways William Hogarth is a representative figure. He was a pioneer of the 'conversation piece', the small-scale informal group portrait, much favoured by the aspirant middle-classes for the walls of their houses. There are several examples of these in the Gallery by artists other than Hogarth, notably The Shudi Family Group by Marcus

George I (1660–1727)
John Michael Rysbrack,
c.1720–35
Terracotta bust, height 629mm
(24¾") (NPG 4156)

Tuscher and *Jonathan Tyers and His Family* by Francis Hayman. Shudi made harpsichords, (his firm later became John Broadwood's, famous as a manufacturer of pianos) and Tyers was the entrepreneur behind the pleasure gardens at Vauxhall.

Hogarth is most celebrated for his *Modern Moral Tales*, the series of images such as *The Rake's Progress* or *Marriage à la Mode* commenting on the dangers of moral corruption inherent in a too slavish following by the middle classes of the taste and mores of the aristocracy. The narrative structure and moral concerns of these graphic stories were echoed in the

Robert Walpole, 1st Earl of Orford (1676–1745)
Studio of Jean Baptiste van Loo, 1740
Oil on canvas, 1257 × 1003mm (49½ × 39½")
(NPG 70)

Walpole, the first statesman to be referred to as the 'prime minister', combined the role with that of Chancellor of the Exchequer, whose robes he wears and whose scarlet purse he displays. His status is further enhanced by the ribbon and star of the Order of the Garter, but it is the sense of Walpole's bulky physique and powerful personality that give this image its force.

William Hogarth (1697–1764)

SELF-PORTRAIT, c.1757

Oil on canvas, 451 × 425mm (17¾ × 16¾")
(NPG 289)

Here is the painter, patriot and moralist as he saw himself, palette and brushes in the left hand, knife in the right, shaven head topped by a velvet cap as he leans eagerly forward to pay a painter's tribute to his inspiration the Comic Muse, which he has already outlined in chalk on the canvas. The position of Hogarth's body and the angle of the easel invite us to share in the process, to recognise that we, the viewers, are part of the comedy, both subject of its narrative and object of its moral lessons. It is a very direct painter's manifesto, proclaiming the balance between craft and intellect, between medium and message, that characterised Hogarth's work.

Thus the painting appears, and very appropriate in its professional respectability for a governor of the Foundling Hospital and recently appointed Sergeant-Painter to the king. Hogarth made etched versions of the portrait, with minor variations, seven times between c.1758 and 1764, so we can assume that he considered it an acceptable image. But underneath is another story, revealed by radiography in 1968 and 1971. Here, Hogarth's body is more upright, seated probably on a stool and closer to the viewer. There is no easel, although the high lead content of the paint used in the later addition of it, being opaque to X-ray, makes it appear prominent. Instead, a nude model or models sit on a platform, posing for one of Hogarth's history paintings which cannot be identified.

This hidden composition is another manifesto, a more aggressive and pungent one than the final image. Here Hogarth asserts his own ability and challenges the dominance of foreign – particularly Italian – painters in the field of history painting. His father-in-law Sir James Thornhill had lost work to them, notably to Jacopo Amigoni, and when Hogarth heard that the Italian was pitching for the commission to decorate St Bartholomew's Hospital, he kept him out by volunteering, as an Englishman, to take on the job free of charge – and was accepted.

To reinforce his personal and patriotic message, Hogarth enlists his *alter ego*, the pug dog. In the bottom left-hand corner of the X-ray the little animal cocks its leg over two framed canvases which we can safely assume represent paintings by foreign masters, a crude scatalogical dismissal of the worth of many such images as shipped back to Britain by wealthy Grand Tourists, or that passed through the picture dealers to the detriment of home-produced art. This canine dimension of Hogarth's self-image – small, fierce, impudent, watchful, faithful to his aesthetic principles, literally dogged – was suppressed in favour of a less polemical, more conventional representation of artistic endeavour.

prose equivalents by Samuel Richardson and Henry Fielding, and the availability of Hogarth's works as modestly priced engravings rendered them accessible to, and influential upon, a much wider range of consumers than previous forms of art.

In portraiture, Hogarth struck a defiantly Anglo-centric pose, even going so far as to sign one of his works *W. Hogarth Anglus pinxit* [painted]. He was incensed by the patronage accorded to artists such as Van Loo and Amigoni, particularly when there were, in his opinion, plenty of competent British painters crying out for work. His manifesto can be seen in his portrait of Captain Thomas Coram, founder of the Foundling Hospital; the Gallery's portrait of William Jones, from the same year (1740), shares its characteristics of directness and lack of pretension. These middle-class Britons, socially flexible, politically free and intellectually vigorous as Hogarth himself, contrasted in his mind with the effete and tyrannised inhabitants of France. Hogarth was a key figure in the establishment of a British cultural identity, which was partly a by-product of the long struggle against our continental neighbour.

John Wesley also defied established beliefs and practices. For him, the Church of England was too remote from the people, too rich and complacent, too comforting in its doctrines to care properly for the souls of its congregations. He led the Methodist movement, enthusiastically taking the living word of God, the hope of salvation and the fear of damnation directly to the people. It is estimated that Wesley preached some 40,000 sermons between 1739 and 1791. The portrait of his sympathiser George Whitefield emphasises the importance of preaching within the Methodist movement, and its effects on the impressionable. By all accounts, Wesley was a charismatic preacher and truly saintly man, and was the mainspring behind the moral evangelism of the eighteenth and nineteeth centuries.

The career of George Frideric Handel, like Hogarth's, exemplified a shift away from sophisticated, international court-based culture to something more definably British. Coming over from Hanover to compose and produce Italian opera, Handel had an immediate success with *Rinaldo* in 1711, and for the next twenty-five years persisted with the genre in the face of many difficulties. One problem for him was the increasing demand for Christian themes expressed in English words, best performed not by the highly paid Italian stars, but by British singers backed by amateur choruses, another cultural expression of the aggressively Protestant British nationalism

John Wesley (1703–91)
Nathaniel Hone, c.1766
Oil on canvas, 1257 × 997mm (49½ × 39¼") (NPG 135)

developing in contrast to the Catholicism of France. Handel's success in infusing his religious oratorios with the drama and emotion of his best operas culminated in his most celebrated work, *Messiah*, commemorated in his portrait by Thomas Hudson (page 56).

Hudson was a Devonian, a thoroughly professional portrait painter running a lucrative London practice from about 1735 to 1755. Joshua Reynolds, a schoolmaster's son and fellow West Country man, was apprenticed to him

Sir Joshua Reynolds (1723–92)
Self-portrait, c.1747–9
Oil on canvas, 635 × 743mm (25 × 29¼") (NPG 41)

in 1740, but after three years of the seven agreed, left his master. For Reynolds, Hudson was too prosaic, too unintellectual: the young man had been developing ambitious ideas for not just the practice of portraiture but for the intellectual and social status of fine art as equal to literature and music. These ideas matured on a trip to Italy from 1750 to 1752. Reynolds brought back, both in sketchbooks and memory, a formidable repertoire of poses which, when blended with his unerring eye for idiosyncrasy, created his reputation for great versatility, best witnessed by Thomas Gainsborough's exasperated yet admiring remark 'Damn him, how various he is!' A glance at Reynolds's portraits in the Gallery of John Stuart, 3rd Earl of Bute, Laurence Sterne, Dr Samuel Johnson and Warren Hastings might support this.

George Frideric Handel (1685–1759)
Thomas Hudson, 1756
Oil on canvas, 2388 × 1461mm (94 × 57½")
(NPG 3970)

Known as the Gopsall Portrait, after the house in Leicestershire of Charles Jennens, librettist of *Messiah*, who commissioned it, this commemorates the life's work of the composer, who was by then blind and aged. It was secured for the nation in 1968 with the help of a special government grant and a public appeal.

Reynolds played a key role in embedding painting in general, and portraiture in particular, in wider British cultural life through his influential role from 1768 as founding President of the Royal Academy of Art in London. This body set professional standards, underpinned intellectually by Reynolds's annual presidential 'Discourses', and provided a prestigious venue for the public display of painting, beneficial to the prospects of artists and providing popular access to their work. The group portrait of Sir William Chambers, Joseph Wilton and Sir Joshua Reynolds by John Francis Rigaud celebrates this institution, which continues to play a major role on the cultural scene.

Reynolds's admiration for the great masters of his day in the written and spoken word led him to seek the society of men such as Samuel Johnson, Oliver Goldsmith and David Garrick. Garrick, the greatest actor of the era, was rich, successful and happily married; the portrait by Reynolds of Garrick and his wife Eva Maria expresses all this. Equally at home in Tragedy or Comedy (another portrait by Reynolds depicts him as torn between the two), Garrick's fame and reputation were greatly enhanced by the number of portraits of him, in role and out, which were engraved and widely sold.

Thomas Gainsborough was a more Bohemian character than the status-conscious, socially ambitious Reynolds. He lived a raffish life: fond of drink, women and carousing with his musical friends, he painted portraits partly to satisfy his wife's budgetary demands. He also produced paintings with a quality of shimmering, ethereal beauty which Reynolds himself, although doubtful about the technique by which they were accomplished – he actually used the word 'daubs' on one occasion – nevertheless recognised as the product of a rare talent. In further contrast to Reynolds, Gainsborough worked alone, eschewing the assistance of drapery painters and other bit-part specialists.

Music was Gainsborough's great love, witnessed in the Gallery's collection by two fine portraits of German musicians resident in London with whom he became intimate. (It is worth pointing out that you do not have to be British-born to qualify for entry to the national collection: the criterion is that you must have contributed significantly to British life while resident here.) Johann Christian Bach (page 60), a son of Johann Sebastian, became known as 'The English Bach'. He and the viola da gamba player Carl Friedrich Abel, both accomplished professionals on the London music scene, enjoyed convivial

David Garrick (1717–79) **and his wife Eva Maria Garrick,**
née Veigel (1724–1822)
Sir Joshua Reynolds, 1772–3
Oil on canvas, 1403 × 1699mm (55¼ × 66⅞")
(NPG 5375)

Reynolds was a friend of the Garricks, and the sittings for the portrait,
mostly taking place in 1772, were occasions for much gossipy conversation.
David and Eva Maria were happily married from 1747 until Garrick's death
in 1779. She, by all accounts a brilliant dancer and woman of 'good sense
and gentleness of manners', had come to England from Vienna.

Johann Christian Bach (1735–82)
Thomas Gainsborough, c.1776
Oil on canvas, 765 × 638mm (30⅛ × 25⅛") (NPG 5557)

music making with Gainsborough, although occasionally finding the artist's modest but very enthusiastic playing a little painful.

Britain's century-long rivalry with France, essentially an economic conflict, was given a keen ideological edge by the French Revolution and the career of Napoleon Bonaparte. The arriviste Emperor – dismissed as 'not a gentleman' by the patrician Arthur Wellesley, 1st Duke of Wellington – was finally defeated by the duke's allied army at Waterloo (1815), but more fundamentally by British capital sustaining anti-French alliances and by the

Horatio Nelson,
Viscount Nelson (1758–1805)
Sir William Beechey, 1800
Oil on canvas, 623 × 483mm
(24½ × 19") (NPG 5798)

Royal Navy's spectacular victories and less glamorous but equally effective blockading. The death of Horatio, Viscount Nelson, at Trafalgar (1805) was the sacrificial culmination to an extraordinary life and career. A fighting admiral of unsurpassed skill and courage, the warmth and humanity shown in his day-to-day leadership endeared him to his officers and crews. His very ordinary failings – vanity, ostentation, even chronic sea-sickness, and above all his love-life involving the sensational Emma, Lady Hamilton – gave his public character a many-layered accessibility never achieved, nor indeed desired, by the more restrained Wellington.

The American (1775) and French Revolutions (1789) had been justified ideologically by assertions that mankind had natural rights to liberty, equality and the pursuit of happiness, which were denied by European monarchical systems. These dangerous views were persuasively articulated by Thomas Paine in *The Rights of Man* (1791–2). Agreeing in principle with Paine's sentiments, but challenged by his limiting title, Mary Wollstonecraft (who married William Godwin) wrote *A Vindication of the Rights of Woman* (1792). This set out radical views, influenced by Rousseau, about greater

Mary Wollstonecraft (1759–97)
John Opie, c.1797
Oil on canvas, 768 × 641mm (30¼ × 25¼") (NPG 1237)

political equality between the sexes: women, communicating to their children at home the moral tenets of citizenship, were thus acting as responsible citizens who should have political rights.

George Gordon, 6th Lord Byron, was a phenomenon encapsulating all that is understood by the terms 'Romantic' and 'romantic'. A product of an age reacting against the detached rationalism of the Enlightenment, he was passionate in both his intellectual response and personal behaviour. To a considerable extent, his brooding good looks defined contemporary fashion for natural, windswept masculinity as opposed to the *soigné* wigs and breeches of the previous age. In an era of war and revolution, his poetry,

George Gordon Byron, 6th Baron Byron (1788–1824)
Thomas Phillips, 1835
Oil on canvas, 765 × 639mm (30⅛ × 25⅛")
(NPG 142)

John Wilkinson (1728–1808)
Lemuel Francis Abbott, 1790s
Oil on canvas, 737 × 616mm
(29 × 24¼") (NPG 3785)

reflecting and commenting, was hugely successful and his engagement
with issues was more than merely intellectual – he died at Missolonghi in
western Greece while supporting the Greeks in their struggle for inde-
pendence from the Turkish empire.

Rich natural resources, good communications, minimal government
interference, an available workforce and a market stimulated by the
demands of war were some of the reasons for Britain's early industrialisation.
It also needed tough, clever entrepreneurs such as John Wilkinson to see
the technological and commercial possibilities and invent the appropriate
systems. Wilkinson's blast furnaces produced not only the iron for weapons
of war, but also the strength behind much of the machinery of the period.
One of the prices paid for this progress was the frequently crowded and
unsanitary living conditions of the new urban working-class. The work of
Edward Jenner, whose observations of the preventative effect of cow-pox
against the killer disease smallpox led to the development of a successful
vaccine (from the Latin *vacca*, a cow), contributed significantly to an
improvement in public health.

The world of Jane Austen was somewhat distant from factory chimneys
and infectious diseases. It was not, however, a hermetic world totally

Edward Jenner (1749–1823)
James Northcote, 1803
Oil on canvas, 1270 × 1016mm (50 × 40") (NPG 62)

isolated from economic and social issues or contemporary intellectual fashions. Captain Wentworth, in *Persuasion* (1818), wealthy from naval prize money, represents the invigorating effect of new money, rendered socially acceptable if sanitised by the ownership or tenanting of land. He contrasts with the effete and corrupt Elliotts, failed 'old money'. Mr Darcy in *Pride and Prejudice* (1813), is a child of Romanticism in his dark moods and eventual adoration of Elizabeth Bennet's freedom of speech and movement.

Jane Austen (1775–1817)
Cassandra Austen, c.1810
Pencil and watercolour,
114 × 80mm (4¼ × 3⅛")
(NPG 3630)

This slight unfinished
sketch by her sister is the
only reasonably certain
portrait of Jane Austen.
It has become, *faute de
mieux*, the face of Jane
throughout the reading
world. Her niece Caroline
Austen wrote: '. . .there is
a *look* which I recognise as
hers – and though the
general resemblance is *not*
strong, yet as it represents
a pleasing countenance it
is *so* far a truth.'

Jane Austen dedicated *Pride and Prejudice* to George, Prince of Wales, later
George IV. He had a genuine appreciation of her work, and despite his
extravagances, was a man of taste and refinement. The balance of history,
however, favours the Duke of Wellington's judgement that George and
his brothers were 'the damnedest millstones ever hung round the neck of
any government'. Their profligate behaviour, at a time of national crisis
when the very existence of royalty was threatened across the channel, was
politically insensitive; as monarch, George's emotional, and *in extremis*,
lachrymose performances in dealing with senior politicians were a strange
way of defending the royal prerogative.

George IV (1762–1830)
Sir Thomas Lawrence, c.1814
Oil on canvas, 914 × 711mm (36 × 28")
(NPG 123)

First Floor

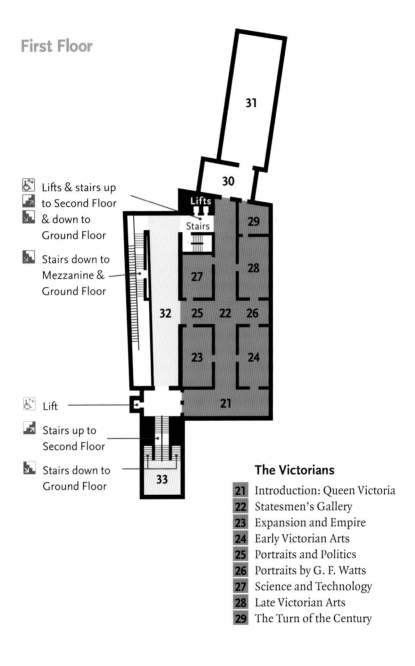

31

30

Lifts & stairs up
to Second Floor
& down to
Ground Floor

Stairs down to
Mezzanine &
Ground Floor

Lifts

Stairs

29

28

27

32

25 **22** **26**

23 **24**

Lift

Stairs up to
Second Floor

Stairs down to
Ground Floor

21

33

The Victorians

21 Introduction: Queen Victoria
22 Statesmen's Gallery
23 Expansion and Empire
24 Early Victorian Arts
25 Portraits and Politics
26 Portraits by G. F. Watts
27 Science and Technology
28 Late Victorian Arts
29 The Turn of the Century

Nineteenth Century: The Victorians

QUEEN VICTORIA is presented to us in Sir George Hayter's portrait as the embodiment of uncorrupted youth, the bright light in a monarchical sky previously darkened by her worldly uncles. Determined from the start to be her own woman, she nevertheless relied on the sage advice of her first prime minister, the avuncular William Lamb, 2nd Viscount Melbourne. After her marriage in 1840 to Prince Albert of Saxe-Coburg-Gotha, an equally wise, although considerably younger man, a source of advice was also available at home. The marriage was a great success in dynastic terms: nine children were produced between 1841 and 1859, whose own marriages and descendants linked Britain to all the major European monarchies. In personal terms, it was a love-match, physically and spiritually fulfilling.

Prince Albert, particularly during Victoria's many debilitating pregnancies, acted as the queen's chief adviser on affairs of State and paid particular attention to the upbringing of the heir to the throne, Prince Albert Edward, later Edward VII. Hoping to produce, in his own image, an intellectual and moral paragon, Albert organised a packed programme of education delivered by carefully vetted teachers. The pupil was unwilling: not a stupid child, very affectionate and with remarkable social skills, Edward's academic performance was consistently disappointing and as he approached adulthood, his susceptibility to the temptations of maturity became all too apparent. The long-term solution was marriage, so enquiries were made into the available Protestant princesses. Despite the difficulties raised by her anti-Prussian family (Victoria and Albert's eldest child Victoria had married the Crown Prince of Prussia), Alexandra of Denmark's youth, sensible personality and good looks won her this doubtful privilege. *The Landing of HRH The Princess Alexandra at Gravesend, 7 March 1863* celebrates the occasion in colourful light-opera style. Prince Albert, though, had died two years previously, and Queen Victoria had begun her forty-year widowhood.

A great consolation, engineered by the Conservative prime minister Benjamin Disraeli in 1876, was to have the title Empress of India conferred upon her. The painting *The Secret of England's Greatness (Queen Victoria Presenting*

a Bible in the Audience Chamber at Windsor) expresses a relationship between Britain and the people of the Empire that Victoria and many of her subjects during the second half of the century would have considered appropriate. Extensive overseas possessions had to be defended against the ambitions of rival imperialists; one of the causes of the Crimean War (1854–6) was the perceived threat of Russian expansion into Asia, specifically endangering India through Afghanistan. The war, remembered for the awesome bungling of senior military officers and the astonishing endurance and bravery of the lower ranks, produced two contrasting popular heroes: James Brudenell, 7th Earl of Cardigan, a sore trial both to his superiors and inferiors, but who courageously led the Charge of the Light Brigade; and Florence Nightingale, whose highly professional reorganisation of the army's hospital services is sometimes obscured by the sentimental image of 'The Lady with the Lamp'. 'The Lady with the Statistics' would more accurately reflect the basis of her achievement.

The expansion of Britain's interests involved the interweaving of a number of processes such as trading, missionary and education work, conquest and exploration. Sir Richard Burton (page 74) was a soldier-turned-explorer who sought to understand the language and culture of the Indian sub-continent and the Arab world, and communicate them to his fellow-countrymen through original works and translations. Sir Robert Baden-Powell (page 75) drew different lessons from his experience as Army officer and colonial administrator, working with and, at intervals, against a variety of Indian and African peoples. He observed the physical inadequacy and lack of initiative of many of the urban working-class recruits for the Anglo-Boer War (1899–1902), and founded the Boy Scout movement to stimulate qualities of self-reliance and outdoor know-how appropriate to an imperial people.

The market for literature expanded steadily throughout the century, stimulated by cheaper printing, easier communications and improved

Queen Victoria (1819–1901)
Sir George Hayter, 1863 after his portrait of 1838
Oil on canvas, 2858 × 1790mm (112½ × 70½")
(NPG 1250)

This painting was bought by Queen Victoria from the artist's executors and presented by her to the Gallery in 1900. The image blends youth and pageantry as the eighteen-year-old queen assumes responsibility for the world's first industrial power. Heraldic symbols evoke Britishness, and the grand setting seems appropriate for an Empress-to-be.

The Mission of Mercy: Florence Nightingale Receiving the Wounded at Scutari

JERRY BARRETT, 1857

Oil on canvas, 1410 × 2127mm
(55½ × 83¾")
(NPG 6202)

The importance of Florence Nightingale's overall contribution to the improvement of the Army's health and welfare provision during and in the half-century after the Crimean War is not in doubt. Recent work, though, questions the immediate benefit of her regime at Scutari, and suggests that her realisation of this failure to lower the death rate in the four months after November 1854 preyed on her conscience after her return. Barrett's painting bathes Florence Nightingale in a saintly light as she makes a Christ-like healing gesture with her right hand; notice, though, that she holds a prosaic notebook in her left hand. Her official notes and letters were formidable: the caring 'Lady with the Lamp' she certainly was to the sick and wounded, but to the army's medical chiefs she must have been more frightening than the Russians. Her analysis of the failings of the military medical system was decidedly unfeminine – by Victorian standards – in its fierce polysyllabic rigour:

> The grand administrative evil emanates from . . . the existence of a number of departments . . . each with its centrifugal and independent action, un-countered by any centripetal attraction, viz a central authority capable of supervising and compelling combined effort for each object at each particular time.

The parlous state of the army's medical services is indicated by the lack of transport for the casualties as they stagger up from the quayside into the quadrangle of the Barrack Hospital at Scutari, just across the Bosporus from Constantinople.

Surrounding Nightingale are a representative group of those who helped, and in some cases hindered, her improvements. Immediately on her left are her supportive friends Charles and Selina Bracebridge, who had guided her early endeavours to obtain professional training and who spent nine months with her in the Crimea. Major Sillery, the tall, bewhiskered figure on the extreme left in the doorway, was so enmeshed in

military medical red tape and his own anxieties, that he was unable even to order the cleaning of the filthy lavatories. Alexis Soyer, on the other hand, on the far left in profile with an umbrella, was a civilian of vigorous and imaginative mind, whose famous culinary skills were recruited by Nightingale to the army's great benefit. The nun discernible to Nightingale's right is the Reverend Mother Mary Clare who led five Bermondsey nuns to Scutari; her saintly character and tactful handling of religious controversy were as important as her nursing skills.

The artist Jerry Barrett appears at the window overlooking the scene, as if to emphasise the evidential reliability of an eye-witness view. This is slightly misleading, as, although he did visit the scene, it was not until July 1856, by which time several of those depicted had gone home. The point of the painting, however, was a general commemoration of the 'Mission of Mercy', rather than a precise documentation of any one occasion.

Sir Richard Francis Burton
(1821–90)
Frederic Leighton, Baron
Leighton, c.1872–5
Oil on canvas, 597 × 495mm
(23½ × 19½") (NPG 1070)

education. The novels of Charles Dickens were sumptuous entertainment, rich in pungent characters and powerful emotions, appearing first as part-works to capture their public, and in later years presented as live readings by the author himself, a man of considerable stage presence and histrionic talent. The portrait by Daniel Maclise (page 76) captures his youthful good looks; as with Alfred Tennyson, 1st Baron Tennyson, revealed as another literary Adonis in the portrait by Samuel Laurence, a later beard substituted gravity for comeliness.

Much of Dickens's work was rooted in the post-industrial urban world; the Brontë sisters, isolated in a North Yorkshire parsonage, relied more on their vivid imaginations interpreting a narrower range of worldly experience. The famous portrait of Charlotte, Emily and Anne by their brother Branwell (page 77), whose ghostly form can be seen lurking half-obscured between the two elder girls, emphasises, in its naïvety, their sisterly solidarity and lack of sophistication. As with the slight image of Jane Austen, the painting is without conventional aesthetic merit, but carries an iconic significance transcending such narrow concerns, and thus is a definitive National Portrait Gallery picture.

One of the prime movers behind the foundation of the National Portrait

Robert Baden-Powell, 1st Baron Baden-Powell (1857–1941)
Sir Hubert von Herkomer, 1903
Oil on canvas, 1419 × 1121mm (55⅞ × 44⅛") (NPG 5991)

Gallery in 1856 was the Scottish historian Thomas Carlyle, who, like many Victorians, ascribed Britain's powerful position to the accumulated achievements of great men and women. Due reverence would be accorded to them, and emulation encouraged by the foundation of a 'Pantheon of all our National Divinities'. Totally in sympathy with this was the painter George Frederic Watts, who was in the early years of his 'Hall of Fame'

The Brontë Sisters: left to right **Anne** (1820–49); **Emily** (1818–48); **Charlotte** (1816–55)
Patrick Branwell Brontë, c.1834
Oil on canvas, 902 × 746mm (35½ × 29⅜") (NPG 1725)

project, an ambitious scheme in which he approached public figures whom he particularly admired and asked to paint their portraits. This resulted in over fifty portraits, a group of which can also be seen at Bodelwyddan Castle, Denbighshire, one of the Gallery's regional partnerships. The paintings are uncompromisingly serious, without the distraction of

Charles Dickens (1812–70)
Daniel Maclise, 1839
Oil on canvas, 914 × 714mm (36 × 28⅛") (NPG 1172)

Thomas Carlyle (1795–1881)
George Frederic Watts, 1868
Oil on canvas, 660 × 533mm (26 × 21")
(NPG 1002)

Carlyle was a harsh, acerbic man and an impatient sitter; the sensitive Watts
was given a rough ride, despite their shared views on the historical
significance of portraiture. Carlyle said Watts had made him look like a 'mad
labourer' (which he was, according to G. K. Chesterton) and told him:
'Mon, I would have ye know I am in the habit of wurin' clean linen!'

Dame Alice Ellen Terry, *Choosing* (1847–1928)
George Frederic Watts, c.1864
Oil on strawboard, 480 × 352mm (18⅞ × 13⅞") (NPG 5048)

William Ewart Gladstone (1809–98)
Sir John Everett Millais, 1879
Oil on canvas, 1257 × 914mm (49½ × 36")
(NPG 3637)

Charles Darwin (1809–82)
John Collier, 1883 (copy after his original of 1881)
Oil on canvas, 1257 × 965mm (49½ × 38")
(NPG 1024)

accessories, aspiring to communicate 'something of the monumental'. While we can agree that, particularly in the case of John Stuart Mill or Cardinal Manning, they truly do this, Thomas Carlyle hated his portrait, saying it made him look, among other things, like a 'delirious old mountebank'. Contrasting delightfully with the predominantly male images is the celebrated painting of the actress Ellen Terry, popularly subtitled *Choosing*. Watts, an unworldly forty-six-year-old, married the sixteen-year old Ellen in the interests of her educational welfare. The marriage lasted one year.

One of the enduring figures of the Victorian, or any age was William Ewart Gladstone. The earliest image of him is in *The House of Commons, 1833* where he sits on the government benches. The later portrait by Sir John Everett Millais dates from 1879, when Gladstone still had thirteen years of active politics to go, including two more terms as prime minister. Millais, a founder-member of the radical Pre-Raphaelite Brotherhood, developed into a successful society portrait painter, capable of appropriate overtones of gravity for senior establishment figures: his portraits of Benjamin Disraeli, Earl of Beaconsfield and of another Conservative prime minister,

Robert Gascoyne-Cecil, 3rd Marquess of Salisbury, bear this out.

Charles Darwin, like Gladstone, was both revered and vilified. His articulation of the theory of evolution, based on extensive scientific observations, challenged narrowly theistic and biblical theories of the origin and development of mankind. Darwin, while displaying the great Victorian intellectual characteristic of empiricism, fell foul of another, the fervent, literal religiosity which subordinated rational argument to biblical authority. Darwin himself was an unenthusiastic polemicist, but Thomas Huxley took up the cudgels on his behalf; the portraits of both men by John Collier reflect this difference of character. While Darwin is elderly, bearded and vulnerable, Collier depicts Huxley as confident, even challenging, and one feels he might use the skull he is portrayed as holding for something other than scientific demonstration if the discussion got heated. His own characterisation of himself as 'Darwin's Bulldog' was well merited.

Darwin and Huxley share space with other key contributors to Victorian scientific progress; portrait makers, in fact, had a new type of hero to commemorate, and with the invention of photography by 1840, a whole new process. The first commercially successful technique for portrait photography was the French daguerreotype. The photographer Richard Beard opened the first commercial studio in Britain, in March 1841, followed in June by

Charles Babbage (1791–1871)
Antoine Claudet, c.1847–51
Daguerreotype, 70 × 60mm
(2¾ × 2⅛") (NPG P28)

Michael Faraday (1791–1867)
Thomas Phillips, 1841–2
Oil on canvas, 908 × 711mm (35¾ × 28")
(NPG 269)

The inventor Faraday's power source was often a battery of the 'trough' type
seen here, developed by William Cruikshank in 1804. The elements of
alternating copper and zinc plates, or *electrodes* (Faraday's term), were
secured to a wooden bar resting on the box filled with a dilute solution of
ammonium chloride. The bar allowed the elements to be removed from the
corrosive liquid when not in use.

Antoine Alphonse Claudet, whose portrait of Charles Babbage enables us to mark, in a suitably innovative way, one of the pioneers of the mechanical calculating machines which were the ancestors of the modern computer.

The effective harnessing of the elemental forces of nature to provide motive power is celebrated in the portrait of Michael Faraday by Thomas Phillips. His work was fundamental to the development of the electric motor; he poses between a battery and a furnace, essential equipment for electrical and metallurgical work. The Gallery owns portraits of several important figures in the railway world, where steam power was as yet the driving force: Robert Stephenson, son of George, was both a civil and a locomotive engineer; Isambard Kingdom Brunel, builder of the Great Western Railway and enormous steam-ships, looking smooth in the painting by John Callcott Horsley, but more jaunty and untidy in the famous photograph by Robert Howlett; and George Bradshaw, without whose guide to the railways the Victorian traveller would have been better staying at home. The social advancement achieved by these energetic men is neatly encapsulated in the image of Sir Daniel Gooch, of the Great Western, whose tiny pair of dividers is the only technical reference in a picture otherwise dominated by two potent items of status display: land and a glossy dog.

The railway system provided easier access to all kinds of products and services, not the least of which was entertainment. Actors, singers, comedians, county cricketers and professional footballers could reach wide audiences and become national figures, either by touring extensively, or by remaining in an increasingly accessible London. Sir William Schwenk Gilbert and Sir Arthur Sullivan, painted by Frank Holl and Sir John Everett Millais respectively, began their famous partnership at the Savoy Theatre in 1871, their mildly satirical jocularity an acceptable pricking of late-Victorian pomposity. Sir Henry Irving and Dame Ellen Terry began their twenty-four-year professional association at the Lyceum Theatre in 1878, as well as undertaking many extensive tours of the provinces. The great stars, as well as domestic touring companies, made use of the European railway system and the transatlantic steamships. Adelina Patti (page 84), a formidable diva with the personality to match her voice, performed in the opera houses of Paris, Madrid and New York, before retiring to a country seat in Wales, where she built her own auditorium and made some of the first phono-graphic recordings, notably her smash hit *Home, Sweet Home*. Oscar Wilde

Adelina Patti (1843–1919)
James Sant, exhibited 1886
Oil on canvas, 1099 × 851mm (43¼ × 33½") (NPG 3625)

had 'nothing to declare but his genius' on arriving in New York. If in the 1890s, your journey became too tedious, you could always shorten it by reading Rudyard Kipling's stories, based on his experiences and observations of British rule in India and its impact on the native peoples; many of these first appeared in an Indian Railway Bookstalls edition. A more beautiful author than the short, bald, bespectacled Kipling was Lady Colin

Henry James (1843–1916)
John Singer Sargent, 1913
Oil on canvas, 851 × 673mm (33½ × 26½") (NPG 1767)

Campbell, née Gertrude Blood, one of the first women journalists, whose sensational divorce case served only to increase the readership of her novels and articles in magazines such as the *Pall Mall Gazette*, *Art Journal*, and *The Ladies Field*.

Creative artists, too, could travel more easily in search of inspiration and clients. The American-born John Singer Sargent was a cosmopolitan figure; brought up by peripatetic, culture-seeking parents who travelled

Europe with their children, he studied in Paris and found success on both sides of the Atlantic and English Channel with his bravura portraits of the great, good, rich and famous. The tense, powerful image of the imperial pro-consul Sir Frank Swettenham reflects Sargent's absorption of the work of Van Dyck, Velasquez and Manet, amongst others, while his versatility is shown in the more subdued but complex study of his fellow American, the writer Henry James. James, like Sargent an ex-patriate American, wrote perceptively about the cultural relationship between Europe and the United States.

It was to France that artists went to study the avant-garde; the experiments with light, paint texture and modes of representation generally known as Impressionism were of great interest to members of the New English Art Club. Seated on the right of their group portrait in the Gallery is the artist Augustus John, whose individual portrait by Sir William Orpen can also be seen. Here we see a true Bohemian, whose exotic life-style, love-life and personal appearance conformed to a popular image of how an artist should look and live. He had a long career as a portrait painter, and in the twentieth-century collection, his economical drawing of T. E. Lawrence and painting of Lady Ottoline Morrell are masterpieces. John was highly critical of his own work, and considered his sister Gwen John the better artist. She, too, lived an unconventional life; for many years the mistress of the French sculptor Auguste Rodin, she painted several self-portraits characterised by ruthless self-examination of her complicated psychological make-up.

Gwen John (1876–1939)
Self-portrait, c.1900
Oil on canvas, 610 × 378mm (24 × 14⅞")
(NPG 4439)

Painted when she was about twenty-four years old, this is the most assertive and confident of Gwen John's self-portraits. The hand on hip, exuberant bow and high, full position within the picture frame contribute to this. The artist's expression is one of watchful superiority. The restricted, yet subtle, tonal range is a demonstration of the sort of skill that led her brother, the painter Augustus John, to value her work above his own.

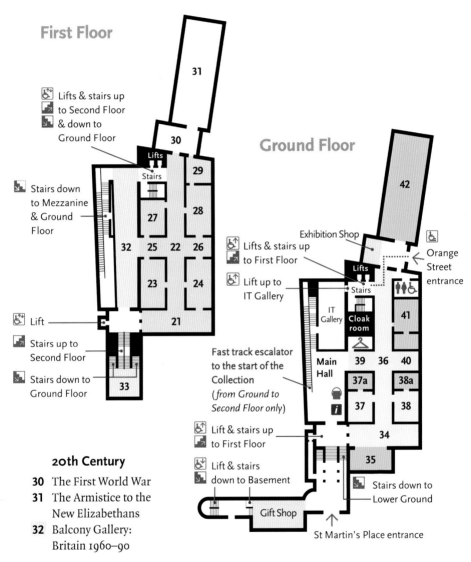

First Floor

**Lifts & stairs up
to Second Floor
& down to
Ground Floor**

**Stairs down
to Mezzanine
& Ground
Floor**

Lift

**Stairs up to
Second Floor**

**Stairs down to
Ground Floor**

Ground Floor

31

30

Lifts

Stairs

29

28

27

25 22 26

32

23   24

21

33

42

Exhibition Shop

**Lifts & stairs up
to First Floor**

**Lift up to
IT Gallery**

Orange
Street
entrance

Lifts

Stairs

IT
Gallery

Cloak
room

41

**Fast track escalator
to the start of the
Collection**
(*from Ground to
Second Floor only*)

Main
Hall

39   36   40

37a   38a

37   38

34

**Lift & stairs up
to First Floor**

**Lift & stairs
down to Basement**

35

**Stairs down to
Lower Ground**

Gift Shop

St Martin's Place entrance

20th Century

30 The First World War
31 The Armistice to the
New Elizabethans
32 Balcony Gallery:
Britain 1960–90

First Floor landing

33 The Royal Family

Britain since 1990

34 Photographs:
popular culture & the arts

36 Contemporaries
37 Late 20th Century Arts
38 Emmanuel Kaye Gallery:
Science, Technology & Business
39 Photographs: public figures
40 Photographs: sporting faces

Twentieth Century
and Contemporary Portraits

T HE FIRST WORLD WAR was a conflict between imperial powers, with soldiers from all corners of the British Empire fighting in France and Belgium, in Mesopotamia and the Gallipoli peninsula. While war memorials to young men went up in towns and villages, the imperial war leaders were commemorated in three large group paintings. These were commissioned and presented to the National Portrait Gallery by the Yorkshire-born South African millionaire Sir Abe Bailey 'to show Bolshevism who led the nations to victory'. *The Naval Officers of World War I* was painted by Sir Arthur Stockdale Cope, *The General Officers of World War I* by an unenthusiastic John Singer Sargent ('The generals loom before me like a nightmare . . .') and the *Statesmen of World War I* by Sir James Guthrie, President of the Royal Scottish Academy (page 90). Guthrie's painting is the boldest, attempting through size, dramatic lighting, expressive poses and classical references, to convey something of the scale of the joint enterprise and its significance in human history. While not going so far as the *Daily Mail* reviewer who said Guthrie had 'achieved a task almost beyond power of human skill', one must agree that it is certainly an impressive performance.

More modest images commemorate several of the young poets who died in the war or who survived to be profoundly marked by their experiences. Rupert Brooke is remembered for his literary evocation of the fervent patriotism which characterised the outbreak of war and stimulated the mass volunteering for the citizen army of Horatio Kitchener, 1st Earl Kitchener of Khartoum. Representing the disillusioned Western Front poets is the self-portrait of the Slade School-trained artist and poet Isaac Rosenberg (page 92), a man of slight build and unmilitary demeanour whose poems, like those of Wilfred Owen and Siegfried Sassoon, represent the protest of an educated class against the physical degradation and mental anguish of trench warfare. Rosenberg's poem 'Louse Hunting' evokes the violence of the battlefield in a description of frenzied de-lousing:

> See gargantuan hooked fingers
> Pluck in supreme flesh
> To smutch supreme littleness.

It is unlikely that regular contact with lice challenged the sensibilities of members of the Bloomsbury Group, whose principled pacifism was given practical expression through their support for the campaign against compulsory military service. The intellectual and aesthetic core of the group began to coalesce from 1904 when Vanessa and Virginia Stephen with their brother Thoby moved into 46 Gordon Square in Bloomsbury, London. Vanessa married Clive Bell, whose friendship brought the painter and critic Roger Fry into the group; Bell had been at Cambridge with the inimitable Lytton Strachey, whose cousin Duncan Grant and friends John Maynard Keynes and Leonard Woolf also became key members of the group, Leonard marrying Virginia. They championed the avant-garde in art and literature, Roger Fry's two exhibitions of French Post-Impressionist art having a far-reaching impact on British aesthetics. A general enthusiasm for the ideas of Sigmund Freud led to an exhaustive interest in dissecting their own motivation, and, in literary terms, was expressed by their admiration for the novels of Henry James. Virginia Woolf declared in 1908 'I shall reform the novel'. Influenced by the dissolution of narrative and formal structure in modern painting, she applied these principles to prose and developed a 'stream of consciousness' technique to record the fleeting thoughts and impressions of an acute sensibility. She was painted by her sister Vanessa Bell as well as by Roger Fry and Duncan Grant; the photograph of her by George Beresford (page 93) has a haunting, angular beauty.

The British monarchy, unlike so many of its European connections, survived the First World War intact, having, in 1917, rejected its family name Saxe-Coburg-Gotha in favour of the British resonance of Windsor. George V was largely responsible for this, responding to popular pressure manifested in the press. From then on, deprived of the moral support of an international system of related royalty, the British monarchy has, of necessity, sought a closer relationship with its subjects, a negotiation influenced by

Statesmen of World War I
Sir James Guthrie, 1924–30
Oil on canvas, 3962 × 3353mm (156 × 132")
(NPG 2463)

The Gallery's archive has a number of photographs Guthrie had taken of himself to set up the poses; this exemplified his deep commitment to the project, as did his study tours to Holland and Spain. The influence of Dutch militia company group portraits, such as those by Frans Hals, and the aristocratic grandeur of Velasquez, can be discerned.

Isaac Rosenberg (1890–1918)
Self-portrait, 1915
Oil on panel, 295 × 222mm
(11⅝ × 8¾")
(NPG 4129)

Private Rosenberg was not much of a soldier, but the acquisition of this portrait by the Gallery, with the support of Edith Sitwell, F. R. Leavis and T. S. Eliot, attests to his stature as a poet. It is a tough image of an awkward, self-absorbed man; it has a calm and concentrated poise, what Siegfried Sassoon called a 'controlled directness'.

vicissitudes ranging from another world war and the loss of the Empire to marital disasters and unexpected death.

George V's eldest son David precipitated the first crisis of the new era of monarchy. As Prince of Wales he had projected a modern image: golf, jazz, trendy clothes and companions as well as a concern for the least fortunate of his future subjects expressed in forceful terms. His outspokenness on social issues was partly a protest against the limitations of his royal status. When he fell in love with the twice-divorced American Wallis Simpson, he chose to challenge those restrictions and insisted, once he became King Edward VIII, that he could not carry on his duties without marrying her. 'An obstinate little man', as Labour politician J. H. Thomas called him, he defied Prime Minister Stanley Baldwin, 1st Earl Baldwin, who made the constitutional difficulties quite clear, received rather quixotic support from Winston Churchill, and less principled support from William Maxwell Aitken, 1st Lord Beaverbrook, who was out to damage Baldwin. Wallis Simpson, as Duchess of Windsor, remained slim and chic until her death. The painting of her by Gerald Brockhurst (page 95) is both stylish and exotic.

The abdication of Edward VIII precipitated the accession of his younger

Virginia Woolf (1882–1941)
George Charles Beresford, 1902
Platinum print, 152 × 108mm (6 × 4¼") (NPG P221)

brother Albert, Duke of York, who took the title of King George VI. A shy and nervous man, he was sustained in his public and private role by the strength and determination of his wife Queen Elizabeth, and took pride in the development of his two daughters, Elizabeth, now Queen Elizabeth II, and Margaret. The dedication of George VI and the regularity of his domestic arrangements restored public respect for the monarchy, as did his example of stoicism and tireless public duty displayed during World War II. The Conversation Piece at the Royal Lodge, Windsor, 1940 by Sir James Gunn reflects this domestic harmony.

Sir Winston Churchill
(1874–1965)
Walter Sickert, 1927
Oil on canvas, 457 × 305mm
(18 × 12") (NPG 4438)

While the monarchy sought constitutional equilibrium, another of
Sir James Gunn's subjects was disturbing the harmony of the natural world
by splitting the atom. Ernest Rutherford, Baron Rutherford, born in New
Zealand, had a long and distinguished career in British and Canadian
universities working on radioactivity and the nuclear theory of the atom.
The charm and informality of his portrait, somewhat belying the awesome
significance for humanity of Rutherford's discoveries, is similar in style to
that of another scientific contributor to the war effort, Sir Barnes Wallis.
Although best-known for his famous dam-busting bomb, his improvements in aircraft design had more lasting significance. More overtly
war-like is the portrait by Sir Frank Salisbury of Field Marshal Bernard Law
Montgomery, 1st Viscount Montgomery of Alamein. The great commander,
scourge of both the Germans and his American allies, poses confidently in
front of a map. The simplicity of the presentation contrasts with the surreal
puzzle of Hein Heckroth's portrait of Sir Basil Liddell Hart, the military
guru and historian.

Wallis, Duchess of Windsor (1896–1986)
Gerald Brockhurst, 1939
Oil on canvas, 1016 × 813mm (40 × 32") (NPG 6416)

This contrast exemplifies a key aspect of the twentieth-century collection, reflecting the incursion of modernist styles and techniques into the traditional field of representative portraiture. The most extreme forms of abstraction, with, for example, a shape or arrangement of colour representing the 'idea' of a person, would not be appropriate to the Gallery's purposes, but there are several interesting examples of semi-abstract images, reflecting the various -isms of twentieth-century art, yet

**Ernest Rutherford, Baron
Rutherford** (1871–1937)
Sir James Gunn, 1932
Oil on canvas, 762 × 635mm
(30 × 25") (NPG 2935)

anchored in representation by recognisable facial features. One such is
Patrick Heron's portrait of T. S. Eliot, which combines cubist interest in
multi-faceted images with a careful study of the shape of Eliot's head, the
whole composition hingeing on his hawk-beaked nose. The result is,
psychologically, intriguingly complex. In this context, one should also
mention the charming double portrait of Ben Nicholson and Dame Barbara
Hepworth by Nicholson, where the outline of their faces is also the key to
the structure of a pattern reflecting their intimacy.

A major cultural development affecting the Gallery's collecting policy,
and the public's expectations of it, has been the expansion and elaboration
of the notion of celebrity during the second half of the twentieth century.
The American artist Andy Warhol (whose dictum that 'everyone will be
famous for fifteen minutes', although clichéd, is an exaggerated encapsulation
of that phenomenon), made a significant artistic comment in his screen
prints of internationally famous women. His Queen Elizabeth II (page 98)
reminds us that the British monarchy has acquired a dimension of international exposure equivalent to that of show-business stars. Part of this
accessibility has been the intense curiosity to which the famous are

Portrait of T. S. Eliot OM: 1949
T. S. (Thomas Stearns) Eliot (1888–1965)
Patrick Heron, 1949
Oil on canvas, 762 × 629mm (30 × 24¾") (NPG 4467)

subjected through the media of press and television, and the intense
scrutiny and analysis of every action and image of them. Charles, Prince of
Wales, relentlessly subjected to this process, was closely associated with the
genesis of the painting of him by Tom Wood (page 99), which projects the
Prince's complex and sensitive nature.

Late twentieth-century politicians have been enthusiastic manipulators
of their personal images as projected through photographs, television,

Queen Elizabeth II (b.1926)
Andy Warhol, 1985
Silk screen print, 1000 × 800mm (39⅜ × 31½")
(NPG 5882/1–4)

Warhol made a series of screen prints of *Reigning Queens* in which the repetitive process of printing is itself a comment on the ubiquity, and in many cases the banality, of images of even the most stellar celebrities. The portraits also emphasise the commodification of individual likenesses in a media-obsessed world, and ask us to think about what this means for royalty.

Charles, Prince of Wales (b.1948)
Tom Wood, 1989
Oil on panel, 1524 × 1575mm (60 × 62")
(NPG L198)

The Prince's love of classical architecture is referred to in this portrait, as are his love of and commitment to preserving the natural environment; the lemon is, one assumes, organic. The shadowy representations of him perhaps refer to other roles he plays, the public and distant aspect of the royal image, or they could symbolise further layers of his personality.

sympathetic press coverage, personal appearances and more rarely, painted portraits. Winston Churchill's famous disapproval of Graham Sutherland's portrait, a gift from the Houses of Parliament which Churchill described pointedly in his acceptance speech as 'a remarkable example of *modern* art', illustrates the potential conflict inherent in an artist-sitter relationship where the sitter is a strong-minded individual with a highly developed sense of his or her place in history, and the artist, unlike the deferential operators of the courtly past, has an aesthetic rooted not in flattery but objective

observation. Although the Sutherland portrait was eventually destroyed at Chartwell, the National Portrait Gallery has a compositional sketch and a preparatory drawing for the head.

Margaret Thatcher, a great admirer of Churchill, is perhaps the most significant British politician of the last thirty years, whose formidable will-power and energy reached parts of her people not normally touched by prime ministers. The monumental scale of Helmut Newton's photograph of her and its harshly dramatic lighting confirms the raw power of her personality. Such an image, produced in collusion with a photographer who understands its visual texture, is a very contemporary response to the decline in respect paid to our elected and hereditary leaders.

When the nation was engaged in world wars or running a world-wide empire, such deference to prominent individuals and institutions supported the system. With the fighting over and, in the phrase of Conservative Prime Minister Harold Macmillan, 1st Earl of Stockton, the winds of change blowing through the Empire, habits of obedience and automatic respect for authority could no longer be guaranteed. A more critical eye could be directed on to those who previously might have been accorded more deference. Out of this shift in attitudes emerged the satire boom of the 1960s, its views and personalities reaching a wide audience through the BBC television programme *That Was The Week That Was*. For a smaller audience, but defining this new mood, was the satirical magazine *Private Eye*, in which the vigorous caricatures of Gerald Scarfe recalled the heyday of James Gillray, Thomas Rowlandson and the Cruikshanks. The National Portrait Gallery has always collected such material, as representing, in a democratic society, a necessary balancing of the more flattering images of conventional portraiture. Scarfe's drawing of Barbara Castle, Baroness Castle (page 102), the forthright Labour cabinet minister of the 1960s and 1970s, is mild compared to his attack on Castle's boss Harold Wilson, Baron Wilson of Rievaulx, or his later savaging of Nigel Lawson, Baron Lawson.

Since 1969, the Gallery has been able to acquire portraits of living sitters. Following a key decision by the Trustees, it has also been able both to commission portraits of contemporary celebrities. This has greatly

Margaret Thatcher, Baroness Thatcher of Kesteven (b.1925)
Helmut Newton, 1991
Bromide print, 1990 × 1140mm (78½ × 45") (NPG P507)

Barbara Castle, Baroness Castle
(b.1910)
Gerald Scarfe, 1975
Pen and Indian ink, 763 × 559mm
(30 × 22") (NPG 6428)

invigorated its functions of both collecting and displaying, enabling it to contribute actively, sometimes controversially, to debates about the definition of celebrity, and to provide active support for traditional notions of representation in art. The Gallery commissions images in all media, from a list of potential sitters drawn up initially by the staff and subsequently ratified by the Trustees. The result may be a single painting, in which the Gallery attempts to broker a fruitful relationship between a famous sitter and a distinguished artist, whose work it wishes to include in the national collection. Popular examples have been Paula Rego's portrait of Germaine Greer (illustrated on page 8), and John Bellany's portrait of Ian Botham. Alternatively, it could be a commission to a photographer to record key members of a certain professional group, such as Barry Marsden's images of famous chefs.

It has become the policy of the Gallery to commission work from leading contemporary figurative artists, for whom the occasional portrait could be seen as a natural extension of their primary artistic interests. The work of Maggi Hambling, for example, features strongly with, among others, portraits of jazz singer and art critic George Melly and the Nobel Prize-winning scientist Dorothy Hodgkin. Hambling's *Self-portrait* (page 104), large, complex and, once decoded, revealing much about her inner self, reminds us also that, while a skilful portrait painter who explores the mental landscape of her distinguished subjects, she also presents herself as their equal, a person of consequence and significance.

Commissioning is pro-active, enabling us to ensure that a balance of areas of endeavour is represented. The portrait of Dorothy Hodgkin, for example, was the product of a deliberate policy to boost the representation of scientists, who as a profession do not appear as often in front of artists and photographers, as say, actors or writers, who have been abundantly

Trade Unionists
Left to right: **Joseph Gormley, Baron Gormley** (1917–93); **Thomas Jackson** (b.1925);
Sidney Weighell (b.1922)
Hans Schwarz, 1984
Oil on board, 1830 × 1830mm (72 × 72") (NPG 5749)

Maggi Hambling (b.1945)

SELF-PORTRAIT, 1977–8

Oil on canvas, 1520 × 1750mm (59⅞ × 68⅞")
(NPG 6562)

Maggi Hambling is a distinguished contemporary painter and sculptor whose portraits in the Gallery's collection include those of Dorothy Hodgkin, A. J. P. Taylor and George Melly. In this self-portrait she explores aspects of her own intellectual and emotional landscape, as she says in her contribution to the Gallery's Sound Guide, recorded in 1997:

> I was spiritually in love with one person, who made the flying teapot and the little clay figures in the upper right-hand part of the picture. And physically with another person, who is visible in the bottom right-hand corner. In the top left-hand corner was my first response to a man I had seen quite by accident in a pub up the road called the North Pole, who was doing card tricks so that people might buy him a drink and of course nobody was buying him a drink. The Brassaï photograph I collaged onto the painting came from a colour supplement, a series of his brothel pictures which I thought was a very beautiful and erotic picture. And the puffer fish being attacked by the adder, I suppose I felt I was a bit of a fish sort of generally puffing myself up but really quite small. And I have three arms, three hands, one for everything you need as an artist. I mean one for the brush, one for the cigarette and one for the drink.
>
> There's confronting the muddle of my life and so when people look at this picture they confront me and my muddle. I mean I quite like that sort of rawness of it. I like things that are raw and I think it has a sense of urgency that it had to be painted.

That reveals most of the mysteries. On 1 August 1999, in the *Independent on Sunday* 'Sitter's Tale' series she added further explanations:

> . . . the leaves of the begonia, the branch of the tree of happiness, were growing by the window in my studio; the tomato at the bottom left was the only tomato I had manged to cultivate all summer. There are autumn leaves sailing into the space at the top and falling out of the bottom. The gulls were swooping about outside, and Concorde always went directly above my studio. I still love Concorde . . . And I have always loved penguins . . . The cat, Onde, considered that chair to be hers, so I'd sit opposite the canvas having to share it with her.
>
> It's a painting made without any attempt at composition. Wherever I made an accidental mark, there had to be something; so the composition just happened, really. I am quite pleased at the way there still seems to be space for the person looking at it to inhabit the canvas, although it is full of all these diverse things.

represented in all periods. With most of the leading politicians of the 1960s onwards included, it was felt that key trade union leaders, powerful political operators in the Harold Wilson 'beer-and-sandwiches-at-Number 10' days, should have their place in the pantheon. Hans Schwarz was commissioned to celebrate the influence of Joseph Gormley, Baron Gormley (miners), Tom Jackson (Post Office workers) and Sidney Weighell (railwaymen) in his painting *Trade Unionists*. A painting of Lord Gormley's successor, Arthur Scargill, unlikely to be similarly enobled, hangs nearby, an abrasive symbol of the decline of trade unionism's political influence.

In the 1960s, Britain lost an empire but gained The Beatles and the Rolling Stones. A vigorous popular culture, mediated through television, popular music, photography, fashion, sport (notably football), newspapers and magazines, has extended the definition of celebrity. For the National Portrait Gallery, registering this cultural phenomenon in both the permanent collection and temporary exhibitions has greatly increased its accessibility and relevance to a wider socio-economic and age range of visitors. Images of Mary Quant, Sir Bobby Charlton, Zandra Rhodes, Geoff Boycott, Dawn French, Jennifer Saunders, the rock group Queen, Sir Elton John and Julie Burchill are as important a part of the contemporary collection as William

Paul Smith (b.1946)
James Lloyd, 1998
Oil on canvas, 1624 × 1451mm
(64 × 57⅛") (NPG 6441)

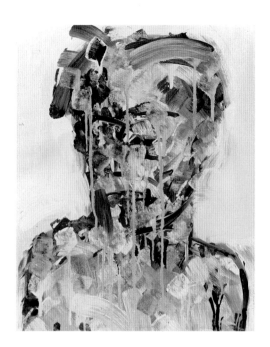

David Bowie (b.1947)
Stephen Finer, 1994
Oil on canvas, 562 × 454mm
(22⅛ × 17⅞") (NPG 6336)

Whitelaw, Viscount Whitelaw, Kazuo Ishiguro, Dame Janet Baker and Tessa Blackstone, Baroness Blackstone.

We might end this survey of our collection by taking a close look at two portraits which, while both of influential contributors to popular culture, are contrasting in their style and technique. Paul Smith is a fashion designer and retailer; his portrait was commissioned from James Lloyd, the winner of the 1997 annual Portrait Award, a competition for young artists which has had a considerable influence in encouraging the continuation of figurative art. It is a bold and engaging image, traditional in its directness of observation and the achievement of a recognisable likeness, yet humorously and irreverently confining the sitter and his professional accessory to a shabby corner of the artist's studio. The portrait of David Bowie by Stephen Finer is more opaque, roughly textured, challenging viewers to draw out of it, or project onto it, their own feelings about the versatile performer whose public persona, unlike the robust Smith's, is characteristically and deliberately unfocused, allowing Bowie the scope to develop and display different facets of his creativity. In their contrasting interpretations of two very different personalities, the artists demonstrate the continuing vigour of the art of portraiture as we enter a new millennium.

Portrait Media at the National Portrait Gallery

NINETEENTH-CENTURY photographs of the Gallery displays show oil paintings, either in serried ranks or, in some of the very earliest hangs, stacked three or four high. Such works still form the majority of images on display, but the visitor of today will notice that a variety of works in other media supplement the traditional oil painting. It is very much the policy of the National Portrait Gallery to *collect* portraits in all media, from grand formal paintings to informal photographs, from prints to marble busts, from miniatures to video portraits. This fulfils our role as an archive of likeness, preserving for posterity all types of images of those who have contributed significantly to British life. It is also our policy to *display* this variety of colour and texture, so people can enjoy a stimulatingly diverse response to a great range of sitters. The following is a brief guide, in very general terms, to the various types of media represented in the Gallery.

OIL PAINTINGS: PANEL AND CANVAS SUPPORTS

Throughout Western Europe during the sixteenth century, the use of oil-based paints for portraits became increasingly important and these were supported by wooden panels. The Gallery has a fine collection of panels displayed in a purpose-built space with the sophisticated environmental controls necessary to keep the wood stable. The panels were made from several planks of wood, typically three or four running vertically for a half-length portrait; the wood used was normally oak, much of it imported from the Baltic. The planks were glued together, although a strengthening batten was sometimes added. Panels were prepared for painting by coating them in layers of gesso, a mixture of plaster made from roast gypsum or alabaster, and size (a thin glue). If you look closely at the Gallery's collection of Tudor portraits, you will see that in most of them, the joins in the

Sir Henry Unton (1557–96)
Detail of portrait illustrated on page 110.

Sir Henry Unton (1557–96)

UNKNOWN ARTIST, c.1596

Oil on panel, 740 × 1632mm
(29⅛ × 64¼")
(NPG 710)

Sir Henry Unton was a Member of
Parliament, Justice of the Peace and
Deputy Lieutenant in his home county of
Berkshire, a representative of that ambitious, hard-working class upon which the
post-Reformation Tudor monarchy
depended for the day-by-day management
of the country. While serving as an ambas-
sador for Elizabeth I in France he died of the
bubonic plague on 23 March 1596. His
death on royal service entitled him, although
only a knight, to the heraldic funeral of a
baron, two rungs higher up the ladder.
Unton's wife, Lady Dorothy, commissioned
this memorial painting to celebrate the
versatility of his achievements and the
status-enhancing grandeur of his funeral.

The picture is a rite of passage from earthly business to the calm of immortality. The composition allows viewers to construct their own version of the narrative within these overall parameters. You might be drawn in to the story by Unton's pale face and dark eyes, then down to the bright elaboration of the tomb and back through his funeral to view his life in flashback – a much-favoured movie format. Or, to continue the cinematic analogy, the activity in his house might serve as an establishing shot leading into the scene where his mother presents him beneath her coat-of-arms as a favoured child, followed by scenes of the young gentleman going to Oxford University, crossing the Channel to further his education

in Italy and soldiering in the Low Countries before dying painfully in France as the doctors desperately bleed him. Back sails his corpse in a mourning ship before the long haul across-country to Berkshire, where sad representatives of all gradations of local society sit under trees on which hang heraldic speech-bubbles saying things like: 'This life grows worse and worse . . . He is dead and gone . . . Never greater grief.'

The painting is described above as *oil on panel*. It is, in fact, painted on three pieces of wood joined horizontally, the smaller lowest one, 93mm high, being of oak (the usual material for panels of this period) and the other two working upwards, 212 and 415mm respectively, being of lime or walnut.

panels are visible. The expansion and contraction of the wood over time can lead to paint loss along these joins.

Canvas replaced wood as the most popular support during the last two decades of the sixteenth century. This can be confirmed by a visit to the Tudor gallery, particularly in the great full-length portraits of Elizabeth I and her contemporaries such as Sir Walter Ralegh and Robert Devereux, 2nd Earl of Essex. The canvas is stretched over and pinned to a wooden frame, known appropriately as a stretcher, then covered with an oil-based ground to isolate it from the paint, too much of which would otherwise be absorbed by untreated canvas.

The basic elements of oil paint have changed remarkably little over the years, and modern methods of production have introduced a wide range of colours. It consists of pigments derived from animal, vegetable or mineral sources, suspended in a vegetable or nut oil (linseed, walnut or poppy were widely used) which will dry and adhere to the support. Before the development of the specialist trade of artists' colourman by the mid-eighteenth century, the raw materials were bought by artists from apothecaries. They then had to be prepared by the artist or assistants, in small quantities to avoid waste by premature drying out. By 1850, the commercial manufacturing of pigments and the invention of the collapsible tube greatly increased their purity and stability, and the convenience of using them.

WORKS ON PAPER

This is a vast subject, comprising everything from modest engravings held in the Gallery's reference collection of prints to unique items such as Ronald B. Kitaj's portrait of Sir Ernst Gombrich. These works are more delicate than the generally robust oil paintings, and require very special treatment for display purposes, as the visitor will observe. Drawings in pencil, chalk or charcoal, for instance, are usually shown in cases, but always with controlled lighting conditions, for limited periods before being 'rested'. While being good conservation practice, this also enables the display to be refreshed at regular intervals with groups of drawings on specific biographical themes. Prints and drawings from the period 1500 to 1840 also have their own dedicated display space within the Gallery.

There is one group of works on paper which performs a vital function in giving balance to our representation of historical figures. This is the

La Promenade en Famille
(William, Duke of Clarence, his mistress Dorothea Jordan and
three little Fitz-Clarences)
James Gillray, 23 April 1797
Hand-coloured etching on paper, 243 × 350mm (9½ × 13¾")
(NPG REFERENCE COLLECTION)

Here we see the humiliation of a Prince of the Blood, as he is forced to
move, because of his extravagance, from Richmond to cheaper accommodation at Bushy. Further shame is evinced by his mistress having to return
to work; the actress Dorothea is learning her lines. Clarence has taken over
responsibility for their unruly brood. Note that chamber-pots were also
known as 'jordans'!

collection of cartoons, made with varying degrees of caricature, mostly of
leading political figures from Oliver Cromwell until the present day. Two
artists stand out: James Gillray's pugnacious, detailed attacks of 1780 to
1810 on royalty and politicians and Gerald Scarfe's merciless excoriation of
the last thirty years of public life. The Gillray hand-coloured etchings –
preserved in several bulky bound volumes – are too unwieldy and delicate
for display, but make regular appearances as slides in the lecture
programme; the Scarfes will make occasional appearances to dent the
reputations of the great and the good.

In contrast to these disrespectful images, the cartoons printed in the
magazine *Vanity Fair* (1869–1910), of which the Gallery has an extensive

collection of the original drawings, are positively affectionate, the graphic equivalent of the gentle contemporary satire of Gilbert and Sullivan's operettas. They have a jaunty, chaffing humour, reflecting male social intercourse amongst the upper and middle classes of late Victorian and Edwardian England, different from the coarseness of Gillray, or from the prolix religiosity of the Cromwellian period. For the historian, this possibility of identifying the distinctive tone of a period through graphic material is very exciting.

MINIATURES

The appeal of portrait miniatures is one of intimacy, of a change of visual mood during a Gallery visit. At intervals in the rooms covering the period 1500 to 1840, the visitor comes across cases displaying some of the most exquisite images in British art. The word 'miniature' derives from the Latin *minium*, the red lead frequently used to highlight the initial letter in the manuscript illuminations of the Middle Ages. (It is a happy etymological confusion that the Latin *minimus* should also mean 'very small'.) The Gallery has a fine group of such works by the Elizabethan artist and goldsmith Nicholas Hilliard (1547–1619), including portraits of the Queen herself, Ralegh, Drake and, in a larger format, Elizabeth's last favourite the 2nd Earl of Essex. Hilliard's *Treatise on the Arte of Limning* (the old word for miniature painting) describes the methods and materials used. The pigments were

Mary Herbert, Countess of Pembroke (1561–1621)
Nicholas Hilliard, *c*.1590
Miniature on vellum,
diameter 54mm (2⅛")
(NPG 5994)

Mary Herbert was the devoted younger sister and literary companion of Sir Philip Sidney and suggested to him the composition of his poem *Arcadia*. After his death in battle in 1586, she took over his patronage of many men of letters, and revised and added to *Arcadia* which was published in 1590. This miniature, like most miniatures of the Tudor period, is painted on vellum stuck down on a playing card.

mixed with water thickened with gum arabic, and applied to a support of 'abortive parchment' or vellum, the burnished skin of a calf. This was stuck on to card to stiffen it (old playing cards were often used). Some areas of colour would be opaque, more thick gouache than transparent watercolour. The exquisite result was enclosed in a frame which, in some cases, was heavily bejewelled.

This remained the basic technique followed in the mid-seventeenth century by Samuel Cooper, described by the connoisseur Cosimo III de 'Medici Grand Duke of Tuscany as 'a tiny man, all wit and courtesy. . .'. Avoiding political controversy, Cooper painted both Oliver Cromwell and his family as well as Charles II and leading royalists. An image of Queen Anne by Charles Boit, dated c.1705, reminds us that enamelled miniatures, where the pigments were fired, enjoyed some popularity. After 1700, artists began to work with thinner colour on ivory instead of vellum, leading to the last flowering of the miniature in the hands of Richard Cosway, who from 1785 was the 'Prince's [of Wales] Principal Painter'.

SCULPTURE

The presence of portraiture in the third dimension is a further example of the visual variety of the Gallery's display rooms. The visitor will find, particularly in the nineteenth- and twentieth-century areas, that portrait sculptures are grouped in islands as well as more formally spaced along the walls. The predominant material is marble, with its smooth monochrome monumentality and classical aura conveying a sense of eternal grandeur. We have fine examples of the works of eighteenth-century masters such as John Michael Rysbrack, Joseph Nollekens and Louis François Roubiliac. This seriousness can occasionally be subverted, delightfully in the case of Lawrence Gahagan's pert bust of Mary Anne Clarke, mistress of the (Grand Old) Duke of York, made in 1811. Plaster casts are also displayed. The pairing of Victoria and Albert as Anglo-Saxons, made to commemorate Prince Albert's death, has a prominent place. Prince Albert's origins in Saxony and the royal couple's love of dressing up in historical costumes are reflected here.

The sculptor must carve a marble image from an obdurate block. Working in terracotta (clay which is later fired) the sculptor models in a more malleable material; or diluting it to produce 'slip', pours it into a mould, itself made of terracotta or plaster. The result is a warm earthy red

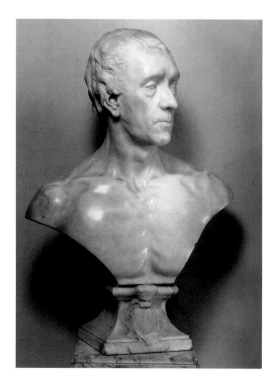

Philip Stanhope, 4th Earl of Chesterfield (1694–1773)
Louis François Roubiliac, 1745
Marble bust, height 578mm
(22¾") (NPG 5829).

colour, kinder to the eye than marble. William Hogarth and George I both appear in the Gallery in this more informal, physically delicate medium.

Bronze is another traditional sculptors' material. An alloy of copper and tin, its surface is capable of holding a variety of gradations of colour and texture. The twentieth-century collection has a strong group of works by Sir Jacob Epstein, their craggy permanence a fine contrast to smooth stone. The portraits of George Bernard Shaw and Ralph Vaughan Williams are characteristic of this. In complete contrast, the beautiful head of Sir William Walton by Maurice Lambert is heavily burnished and the patination gives it an eerie, greenish tinge.

In the later twentieth-century collection, you can normally see sculpture in two further materials: resin and ceramic. Andrew Logan uses resin, and his sculptures of Zandra Rhodes and Lynn Seymour show the expressive possibilities of the medium, enhanced by an imaginative, even flamboyant use of colour. In contrast, the ceramic portraits by Glenys Barton – of which the appropriately double-headed portrait of the Oscar-winning actress turned politician, Glenda Jackson, is an example – are more classical and restrained.

PHOTOGRAPHY

Although the first photographs entered the collection early in the twentieth century, it is only since the 1960s that the Gallery has acquired an international reputation for its collection and exhibitions. The earliest portrait photographs on display date from the 1840s, and are shown under similar conditions to the miniatures they largely displaced.

The first photographic process to be commercially successful was the daguerreotype. This was made by exposing a highly polished silver surface on a copper plate, sensitised by fumes from iodine. It produced a unique positive image, so reproduction was not possible. The Gallery's images of the computer pioneer Charles Babbage and railway engineer Robert Stephenson are examples. This technique proved a dead-end, and was eclipsed during the 1850s by the negative-to-positive processes, the most successful of which was where the negative was a glass plate treated with a mixture of gun-cotton and ether, known as collodion, and dipped in silver nitrate. Still wet, it was exposed in the camera, developed and printed on to paper coated with albumen (egg white). Multiple positive prints could be produced. The photographs of Roger Fenton, who worked under difficult conditions during the Crimean War against Russia (1854–6), shows what could be achieved. In 1878, the inconvenient necessity for wet plates was removed by fixing the sensitive material in dry gelatin.

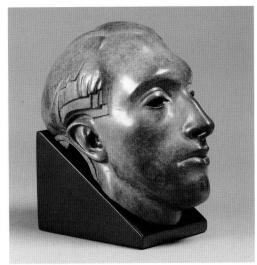

Sir William Walton (1902–83)
Maurice Lambert, c.1925
Bronze, height 270mm
(10⅜") (NPG 5913)

Ian Wright (b.1963)
Tim O'Sullivan, 1994
Black and white print from an original 'R' Type colour print, 304 × 405mm (12 × 16") (NPG X87321)

If some of Fenton's work could be categorised as photo-journalism, the aesthetic possibilities of photography were explored by early photographers such as Julia Margaret Cameron, Charles Lutwidge Dodgson ('Lewis Carroll') and David Wilkie Wynfield. The Gallery usually displays examples of their work but, as original prints are delicate, they can only be shown for short periods. On a more commercial level, another French invention was the use of multiple-lens cameras to enable up to eight separate portrait images to appear on one plate; the result was the carte-de-visite, cheap and easily disseminated, the biggest populariser of photographic images until

Oscar Wilde (1854–1900)
Napoleon Sarony, 1882
Albumen panel print, 305 × 184mm (12 × 7¼")
(NPG P24)

Napoleon Sarony's studio was at Union Square, New York City. Wilde, in America for a series of lectures on 'Art for Art's Sake', commissioned publicity photographs. Sarony called Wilde 'A picturesque subject indeed!' This is borne out by his dandified dress, and enhanced by Sarony's appropriately theatrical backdrop.

The Actress
Julie Walters (b.1950)
Marty St James and Anne Wilson, 1990
Video portrait, duration 21 minutes
(NPG REFERENCE COLLECTION)

rolled film in the late 1880s. Camille Silvy's studio, for example, received up to thirty sitters a day during peak periods in the early 1860s.

The visitor can see photographs in the twentieth-century displays either integrated with other media, or in separate groups thematically arranged according to the profession of the sitters: for example, cooks, architects, actors or business people. There are also displays which give the photographer primacy, where the Gallery draws on its extensive holdings of the works of key figures such as Sir Cecil Beaton, Dorothy Wilding or David Buckland. This extensive exposure of the Gallery's own collection is complemented by regular exhibitions of the work of leading European and American photographers, from Henri Cartier-Bresson to Annie Leibovitz. The Gallery now has a reputation as a key venue for exhibitions and as a patron of contemporary British photographers.

NEW MEDIA

The Gallery is committed to exploring the possibilities of new media and has started a collection of portraits using video and computer technology. The most striking of these is a multi-screen image of the Olympic gold-medal-winning swimmer Duncan Goodhew, by Marty St James and Anne Wilson, in which the linking and overlapping of the movement across the various screens echoes the rippling of the water and the swimmer's fluid movements. It is a very large installation, requiring an entire closed space to accommodate the screens and ensure an ambience sympathetic to the sound that is integral to the piece. The same artists produced the video portrait of the versatile actress Julie Walters, for a single screen, exploring her facial expressions and head movements.

PICTURE FRAMES

Frames both protect and contribute to the visual impact of paintings. They may emphasise the difference of a painting to its surroundings, focusing the eye and commanding attention; or by echoing the decorative or architectural style of the space, help the painting to blend into an overall aesthetic scheme. The Gallery, driven by its chronological imperative, usually frames portraits in styles appropriate to the various periods, so that the frames themselves can be studied as one aspect of stylistic development.

Bulstrode Whitelock (1605–76)
Unknown artist, 1634
Oil on canvas, 762 × 635mm (30 × 25")
(NPG 4499)

This portrait of the Parliamentarian and writer was framed soon after
acquisition in 1966 in a carved silver-gilt frame. It was reframed in 1983 in
this black-and-gold appliqué frame with gilt carved foliage ornament
applied to a flat ebonised black frame – a style popular in the seventeenth
and early eighteenth centuries.

Some of these frames may be original to the portraits, but they often have to be bought from specialist dealers, or made as reproductions. Curators must decide when a frame, made as a reproduction by our Victorian predecessors, is in itself suitably 'historic' to be used. This applies particularly to some of the Gallery's black-and-gold ebonised 'Tudor' frames. Generally, the tendency now is to accept the period effects of Victorian frames, but when a new frame is required, to recreate it with historical accuracy.

A particular skill of the Gallery's framemakers is their ability to exercise all the techniques of imitating carved wood, vital since carved wood frames became too expensive to be in demand; and artificial ornament came to be widely used. 'Compo' is a composition of whiting, glue, resin and linseed oil. Skilfully applied and then gilded, it cannot be easily distinguished from wood. However, it is a fragile substance, so many frames embellished by it pass through the framers' workshop for repair.

CONSERVATION

In the last twenty years the Gallery has made significant improvements to the air-treatment systems controlling the environment in the main permanent display and temporary exhibition galleries. The Studio Gallery, for instance, was too unstable an atmosphere for panel paintings until recent work stabilised its temperature and humidity. Computerised monitoring is now general, and overcomes changes in weather and the heat given off by humans! The lighting, too, is now more sophisticated and adaptable to the relatively high level tolerated by oil paintings, and the more subdued levels appropriate to works on paper.

In addition to the display areas, the Gallery has also improved the storage conditions for all types of material. The Archive and Library, opened in 1993, with its environmentally stable storage areas for documents, photographs, prints and drawings, finally ended the somewhat peripatetic existence the Gallery's reference facilities had endured over the previous thirty years, at one time in Carlton House Terrace, followed by a period in Lewisham. The paintings store is now based at Merton, releasing more display space in the main building.

The Conservation Studio was also opened in 1993, thanks to the generosity of the Headley Trust. The Studio is staffed by a team of freelance conservators who have all been with the Gallery for many years. Decisions

Sir Nathaniel Bacon (1585–1627)
Self-portrait, c.1625 (*during conservation*)
Oil on panel, 575 × 445mm (22⅝ × 17½") (NPG 2142)

about conservation work on particular paintings are taken by the relevant curators after consultation with the conservators. A particularly dramatic example concerned a portrait of the gentleman artist Sir Nathaniel Bacon, which was obscured by dirty and discoloured varnish. A thorough examination revealed that the right-hand quarter of the portrait was not original. It transpired that at some time in the past all the original paint had

Sir Nathaniel Bacon (1585–1627)
Self-portrait, *c.*1625 (*after conservation*)
Oil on panel, 575 × 445mm (22⅝ × 17½") (NPG 2142)

been scraped off in that area, probably because it was flaking.
The overpaint, which was clumsy and unconvincing, was removed during
the cleaning process and that part of the portrait was carefully
reconstructed with reference to a contemporary copy of the original.

Index

Second Floor

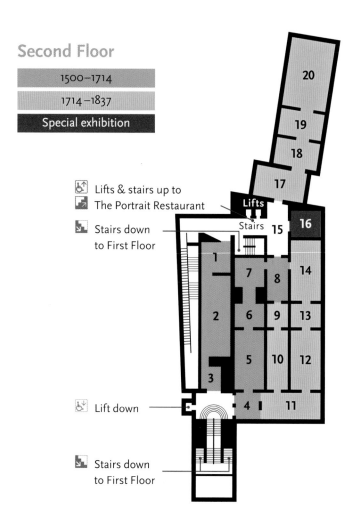

1500–1714

1714–1837

Special exhibition

Lifts & stairs up to
The Portrait Restaurant

Stairs down
to First Floor

Lifts

Stairs

Lift down

Stairs down
to First Floor

Tudor Galleries

1 The Early Tudors
2 The Elizabethan Age
3 Miniatures Gallery

17th Century

4 The Jacobean Court
5 Charles I and the
Civil War
6 Science and the Arts in
the 17th Century
7 Charles II: The
Restoration of the
Monarchy
8 The Later Stuarts

18th Century

9 The Kit-cat Club
10 The Arts in the early
18th Century
11 Britain in the early
18th Century
12 The Arts in the later
18th Century
13 Science and Industry
in the 18th Century
14 Britain becomes a
World Power

Late 18th and early
19th Century

17 Britain at War
1793–1815
18 The Romantics
19 Science and Industry
in the early 19th
Century
20 The Regency

First Floor

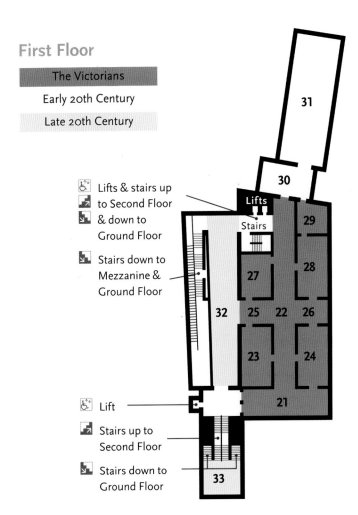

The Victorians

Early 20th Century

Late 20th Century

Lifts & stairs up
to Second Floor
& down to
Ground Floor

Stairs down to
Mezzanine &
Ground Floor

Lift

Stairs up to
Second Floor

Stairs down to
Ground Floor

Lifts

Stairs

31

30

29

28

27

32

25 22 26

23 24

21

33

Ground Floor

Britain since 1990

Special exhibition

Gift Shops

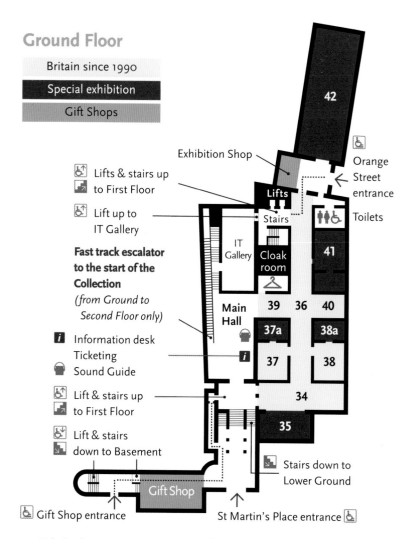

42

Exhibition Shop

Orange
Street
entrance

Lifts & stairs up
to First Floor

Lifts

Lift up to
IT Gallery

Stairs

Toilets

IT
Gallery

**Fast track escalator
to the start of the
Collection**
*(from Ground to
Second Floor only)*

Cloak
room

41

39 36 40

Main
Hall

37a

38a

i Information desk
Ticketing
Sound Guide

37

38

Lift & stairs up
to First Floor

34

Lift & stairs
down to Basement

35

Gift Shop

Stairs down to
Lower Ground

Gift Shop entrance

St Martin's Place entrance

Britain since 1990

34 Photographs: popular
culture & the arts

36 Contemporaries

37 Late 20th Century Arts

38 Emmanuel Kaye
Gallery: Science,
Technology & Business

39 Photographs:
public figures

40 Photographs:
sporting faces

Special Exhibitions

16 Room 16 (*Second Floor*)

35 Porter Gallery

37a Room 37a

38a Room 38a

41 Room 41

42 Wolfson Gallery

43 Clore Studio Gallery
(*Lower Ground*)

44 Book Shop Gallery
(*Basement*)

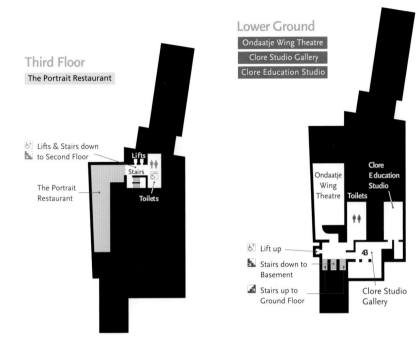

Third Floor

The Portrait Restaurant

Lifts & Stairs down
to Second Floor

Lifts

Stairs

The Portrait
Restaurant

Toilets

Lower Ground

Ondaatje Wing Theatre
Clore Studio Gallery
Clore Education Studio

Ondaatje
Wing
Theatre

**Clore
Education
Studio**

Toilets

Lift up

Stairs down to
Basement

Stairs up to
Ground Floor

43

Clore Studio
Gallery

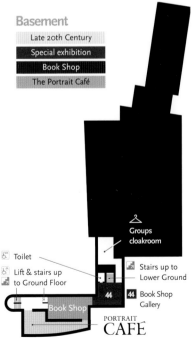

Basement

Late 20th Century

Special exhibition

Book Shop

The Portrait Café

Groups
cloakroom

Toilet

Lift & stairs up
to Ground Floor

Stairs up to
Lower Ground

44

44 Book Shop
Gallery

Book Shop

PORTRAIT
CAFÉ

General Information www.npg.org.uk

Opening hours

Monday–Wednesday, Saturday and Sunday: 10.00–18.00; Thursday and Friday: 10.00–21.00. The Gallery is closed on the 24–26 December, 31 December, 1 January and Good Friday. The shops close 15 mins before the Gallery on Thursday and Friday evenings.

Access for disabled visitors

Disabled access is situated at the Gift Shop entrance, St Martin's Place, and at the Orange Street entrance. Wheelchairs and lifts are available in the Gallery for visitors with mobility difficulties. For visually impaired visitors, a touch tour and Braille information panels are available.

Gift Shop

The Gallery's ground-floor Gift Shop carries a wide range of gifts based on the Gallery's collection, from posters and postcards to stationery, jewellery, watches and picture frames. The award-winning Portrait Printer service enables visitors to buy a high-quality reproduction of almost 10,000 portraits in the Gallery's main collection.

Exhibition Shop

Situated outside the Wolfson Gallery, the Gallery's main exhibition space on the ground floor, the Exhibition Shop specialises in books and gifts to accompany the Gallery's major exhibitions.

Book Shop

The basement Book Shop, situated in the original brick vaults of the Gallery, specialises in titles on British history, art, portraiture, photography, costume, literature and biography. It also carries the complete range of the National Portrait Gallery's own publications.

Refreshments

The Portrait Café serves a range of light meals and refreshments and is located in the basement, adjacent to the Gallery Book Shop. The Café is open from 10.00–17.30 Monday–Wednesday, Saturday and Sunday and from 10.00–20.30 Thursday and Friday. The Portrait Restaurant, on the Gallery's top floor, offers the best in contemporary British cuisine against the backdrop of spectacular views across central London. The Restaurant is open from 10.00–17.30 Monday–Wednesday, Saturday and Sunday, and from 10.00–22.00 Thursday and Friday (last orders 20.30).

Sound Guide

The National Portrait Gallery Sound Guide provides visitors with a recorded history on CD-Rom of over 200 famous portraits on display in the Gallery, including actual recordings of many of the great men and women of the late 19th and 20th centuries. A 'highlights' tour, of fifty portraits, is also available in French, Spanish and Japanese.

IT Gallery

The Woodward Portrait Explorer, located in the IT Gallery on the ground floor (mezzanine), enables visitors to take a virtual tour of the Gallery's collection through the use of 11 dedicated touchscreens.

Heinz Archive and Library

Located in the Gallery's administrative building, opposite the Orange Street entrance, the Heinz Archive and Library contains primary reference material on the history of British portraiture, including an extensive collection of prints, drawings and photographs. There is also a comprehensive reference library as well as key periodicals and catalogues of exhibitions, permanent collections, dealers and auctioneers. The public study room is open by appointment, Monday 11.00–17.00, Tuesday–Friday 10.00–17.00. Closed Bank Holidays and 24 December–1 January inclusive, and 2 week annual stocktake.

Picture Library

The Picture Library manages the Gallery's copyrights and supplies images for use in books, magazines, TV and many other projects. A comprehensive research service, photography and rights licensing is provided to professional clients. The department also sells hand-finished photographic prints.

Education Department

The Education Department organises a wide range of activities and workshops for both adults and young people, taking place either in the Gallery or in the department's well-equipped studio and adjoining darkroom. The 150-seat Ondaatje Wing Theatre offers excellent facilities for regular public lectures and seminars.

Regional Partnerships

The Gallery enjoys a number of regional partnerships with country houses open to the public outside London. Works from the Gallery's collections are displayed at the following National Trust properties: Montacute House, Somerset; Gawthorpe Hall, Lancashire; and Beningbrough Hall, Yorkshire. There is a further selection of works at Bodelwyddan Castle, in North Wales, administered by Clwyd Council.